# ANCIENT EGYPT

WHITE STAR

PUBLISHERS

# ANCIENT EGYPT

**TEXT**
Giorgio Agnese
Maurizio Re

**EDITORIAL PRODUCTION**
Fabio Bourbon
Enrico Lavagno

**GRAPHIC DESIGN**
Paola Piacco

**TRANSLATION**
Neil-Frazer Davenport

## Contents

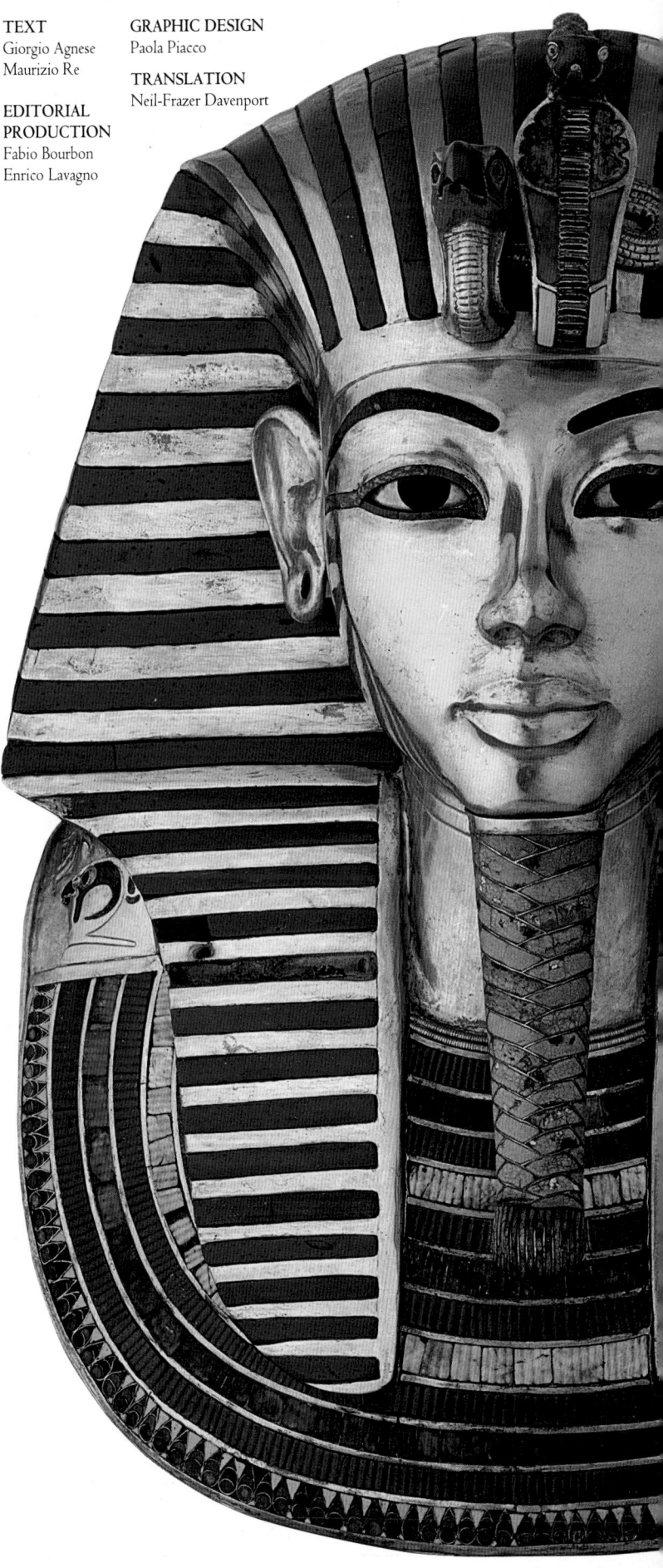

*1 One of the colossi of Rameses II in the temple at Luxor.*

*4 A colossus head of Rameses II in the temple at Luxor.*

*2-3 The Sphinx and the Pyramid of Khafre at Giza.*

*5 The solid gold death mask of Tutankhamun.*

© 2001 White Star S.r.l.
Via Candido Sassone, 22-24
13100 Vercelli, Italy

Distributed in Egypt by
*White Star Egypt* -
Plaza Mall 9 - Units 5/6 - Naama Bay
Sharm el-Sheikh, South Sinai, Egypt
Tel. (+20)069/601277
Fax (+20)069/600135
e-mail: wsegypt@whitestar.it

ISBN 88-8095-617-5
1 2 3 4 5 6  05 04 03 02 01

Printed in Italy.

QATTARA
DEPRESSION

*Libyan Desert*

OASIS OF BAHARIYA

# EGYPT

**6 top left**
*A fleet of feluccas sailing on the Nile.*

**6 bottom left**
*An aerial view of the Nile near Luxor.*

OASIS OF
DAKHLA

*Lybia*

**6 top right**
*The temple of al-Dakke, reconstructed on the shores of Lake Nasser.*

**6 bottom right**
*The oasis of El Feiran, overlooked by Gebel Tahuna, in the Sinai peninsula.*

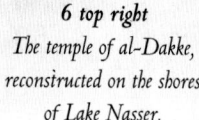

*Sahara Desert*

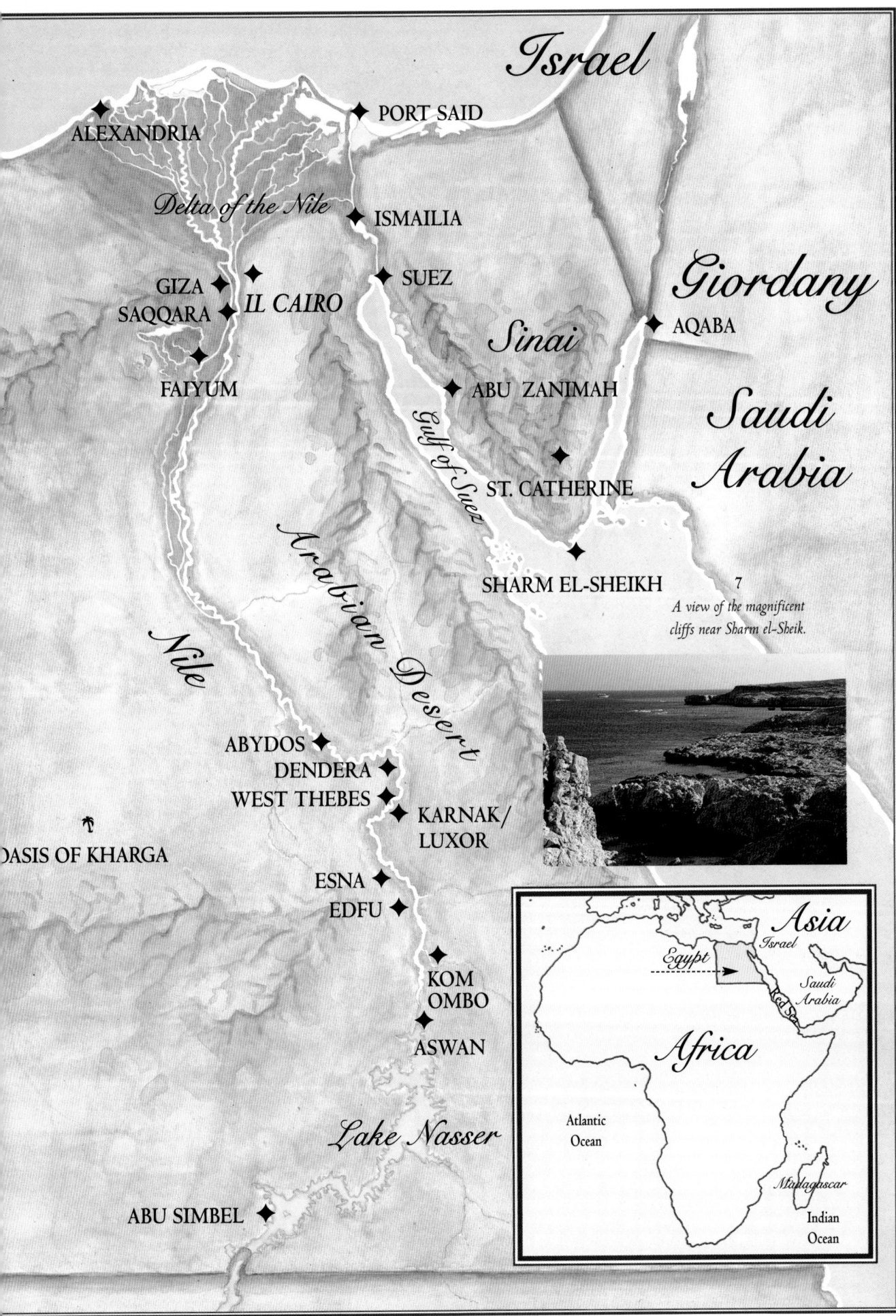

Israel

PORT SAID

ALEXANDRIA

*Delta of the Nile*

ISMAILIA

Giordany

GIZA

SUEZ

SAQQARA

IL CAIRO

AQABA

*Sinai*

FAIYUM

ABU ZANIMAH

Saudi
Arabia

*Gulf of Suez*

ST. CATHERINE

*Arabian Desert*

SHARM EL-SHEIKH

7

*A view of the magnificent
cliffs near Sharm el-Sheik.*

*Nile*

ABYDOS

DENDERA

WEST THEBES

KARNAK/
LUXOR

OASIS OF KHARGA

ESNA

EDFU

Asia

*Israel*

*Egypt*

*Saudi
Arabia*

KOM
OMBO

Africa

ASWAN

Atlantic
Ocean

*Lake Nasser*

*Madagascar*

ABU SIMBEL

Indian
Ocean

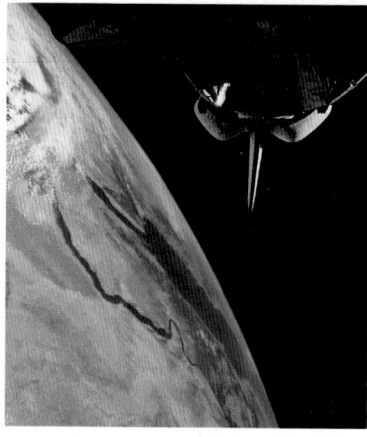

8-9
*This view from space shows the luxuriant Nile Valley: the meander in the foreground corresponds to the Luxor area.*

8 bottom
*Another two views from space in which the Red Sea (left) and the Sinai peninsula (right) are clearly visible.*

# Preface

For obvious practical reasons, condensing into a small volume all the information of general interest concerning Egypt—without neglecting important facts—is by no means easy. Prepararing a concise yet exhaustive text dealing with Egyptian archaeology is all the more arduous given the number and vastness of the sites and monuments found in the country and the fact that the ancient civilisation lasted for over 4,000 years. The selection of sites included in this book comprises all the major tourist attractions, while the historical-archaeological aspects of the monuments mentioned are treated at some length.

The territory inhabited by the ancient Egyptians is that which we see today, consisting of the Nile valley between the Mediterranean to the north and the second cataract south of Abu Simbel. The river traces a fertile strip over a thousand kilometres long. This strip is delimited either side by desert areas which are in turn flanked by arid hills and mountain ranges separating it from the Red Sea to the east and the Sahara to the west. In the north, close to modern-day Cairo, and in proximity to ancient Heliopolis and Memphis, after having flowed for 6,500 kilometres the great river branches out into the delta that in ancient times was green with vegetation but swampy and impracticable. Before the building of the Aswan dam, in fact, the river rose annually, flooding the countryside and leaving the prevailing winds and the sun with the task of drying out land which would emerge covered with a new layer of silt rich in humus and mineral salts.

The lifestyle of the inhabitants of the Nile valley was essentially agricultural; still today, sailing upstream from Cairo the landscape you encounter is little different to the one that existed thousands of years ago. *Kemet* was the name the ancient Egyptians gave to their land: black land, fertile land, the gift of the gods and the deified river Nile.

This ancient civilisation which survived for millennia, was rediscovered and studied in depth only relatively recently. We already know much, but archaeology still has plenty to reveal and Egyptology still has to provide us with answers to questions regarding several obscure periods in its history and numerous unresolved mysteries.

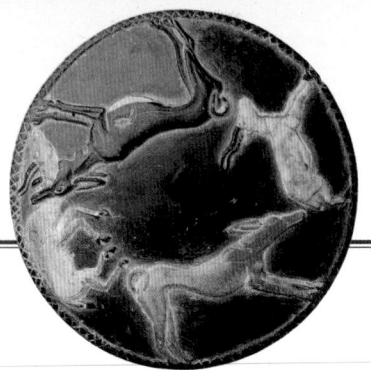

# Historical Introduction

I n 1998, the Egyptologist Guenter Dreyer, from the German Institute of Cairo, discovered two bone tablets at Abydos, in the tomb of an ancient sovereign known to the Egyptologists as the "Scorpion King". The two tablets carry a form of archaic writing and are datable to around 3400 BC, while the Narmer Palette, previously considered to be one of the earliest documents of Ancient Egypt, has instead been dated to 3000 BC.

Given that the culture of ancient Egypt was not actually extinguished until around AD 400, when the knowledge of hieroglyphic writing was lost and the pagan cults were banned from the country, the Egyptian civilisation lasted around 4,000 years, an episode unique in human history.

The area of ancient Egypt had been inhabited from the prehistoric period. In the post-glacial era only two geographical zones were particularly favourable to the development of a civilisation. One of these was the upper valley of the Nile, extending to the south of Africa, the second comprised present-day Turkey and Mesopotamia and extended as far as the Indus River.

The first Neolithic agricultural communities settled in the upper Nile valley and the oases around 7-8,000 years ago. These cultures, defined as "predynastic" enjoyed a rapid organisational, social and technological (metallurgy) development before the start of the dynastic epoch inaugurated with the first historical pharaoh Menes (Aha) who, tradition has it, unified a country hereto divided into northern and southern sectors.

The reality was rather more complex. Archaeological finds testify to the existence of a nameless king (known as the "Scorpion King" after the figure appearing on a ceremonial mace) who reigned at the end of the predynastic period between 3150 and 3050 BC. Many Egyptologists place the Scorpion King in the so-called Dynasty 0 along with Narmer, perhaps the father of Menes. The Museum of Cairo contains the votive Narmer Palette, the

*12 top*
*A steatite disc from the tomb of Hemaka at Saqqara. 1st Dynasty.*

*12 centre left*
*Top, a fragment of the Libyan Tribute Palette, from Abydos, Protodynastic Period; bottom, jar with painted decoration, Predynastic Period.*

most famous find related to this king, discovered at Hierakonpolis (the ancient city of Nekhet) by the American archaeologist Quibell in 1897.

According to Herodotus (whose writings are supported by archaeological research), the pharaoh Menes is attributed with the construction of Memphis, the capital of the unified kingdom at the apex of the Nile delta. The city was protected by a dam designed to deviate the course of the river and avoid the annual flooding of the houses. It is interesting that the kings of this dynasty chose Abydos as their burial ground, the necropolis of the first capital of the country, Thinis. The aristocracy instead had their tombs built at Saqqara. Aha's tomb at Abydos is located in the north-western necropolis, together with that of his presumed wife Benerib.

were frequently exploited and kept in poverty. The discontent this generated inevitably led to increasingly serious internal struggles and a complete undermining of the sovereign's authority. In what was now an ungovernable country, a new feudal-style system was developing. This period included the 7th-10th Dynasties (2152-2065 BC) and is defined as the First Intermediate Period. It was not until the 12th Dynasty and the reign of the pharaoh Amenemhat I (1994-1964 BC) that central power was reinforced at the expense of the sacerdotal class: the capital was moved to It-towi (not far from Lisht) and work began on the expansion of the irrigation system at Fayum. There followed the period of the Senusret I, Amenemhat II and Senusret II and III who extended

*14*
*Diorite statue of Khafra, from Giza. 4th Dynasty.*

*15 top left*
*Ivory statuette of Khufu, from Abydos. 4th Dynasty.*

*15 bottom right*
*Triad of Menkaura in grey-green schist, from Giza. 4th Dynasty.*

The 3rd Dynasty (2649-2575 BC) opened with the pharaoh Sanakht (Nebka) who is less well known than his presumed brother Djoser, the builder of the step pyramid in the central sector at Saqqara (circa 2600 BC). In reality this monument was designed and built by the vizier Imhotep, something of the Leonardo da Vinci of his era and elevated to almost divine status by subsequent generations.

We have far more information about the 4th Dynasty thanks to archaeological finds. The period saw the reigns of the pyramid-building pharaohs Sneferu, Khufu, Khafre and Menkaura, and was one of the most remarkable epochs in history, with Egypt distinguished by an elevated level of social, cultural and artistic organisation. The pharaoh was at the top of the hierarchical pyramid, with the sacerdotal class wielding great political power a step lower. For administrative purposes, the territory was divided into regions known as nomes, and entrusted to members of the aristocracy, the nomarchs. With the passing of time, the sacerdotal class and the sub-divided wielders of temporal power acquired increasing autonomy with respects to the central power of the sovereign and did not always exercise their power over the population correctly. The people

**16 top left**
*Painted limestone pillar of Senusret I, from Karnak. 12th Dynasty.*

**16 bottom left**
*Osiris pillar of Senusret I in painted limestone, from Karnak. 12th Dynasty.*

**16 top right**
*Statuette of a sovereign in painted wood, from Lisht. 12th Dynasty.*

**16 bottom right**
*Painted sandstone statue of Mentuhotep II, from Deir al-Bahari. 11th Dynasty.*

**17 top**
*Pectoral in gold and
semi-precious stones
belonging to Mereret,
from Dashur.
12th Dynasty.*

**17 left**
*Necklace with pectoral in
gold and semi-precious
stones, from Dashur.
12th Dynasty.*

**17 top right**
*Reverse side of the same
pectoral in solid gold.*

**17 bottom right**
*Scarabs of Amenemhat II
in amethyst, from Dashur.
12th Dynasty.*

the Egyptian borders towards the Near East and conquered Nubia with its rich deposits of gold.

The Middle Kingdom (2065-1650 BC) was a particularly fertile period for sculpture, the working of gold, civil and military architecture and, above all, literature; the texts from this epoch were, in fact, copied by the successive generations and the Egyptians themselves referred to this as a "golden age". It is no coincidence that the celebrated novel by Mika Waltari, Sinhue the Egyptian is set in this period of splendour.

Literature, above all, enyoed considerable development and the texts of the period were copied by the successive generations. The works produced during the Middle Kingdom frequently contained intellectual concepts handed down from the Old Kingdom, a fact which has allowed modern scholars an insight into the most remote aspects of Ancient Egyptian knowledge.

The applied sciences also found fertile terrain in the Middle Kingdom and specialist medical, mathematical and veterinary treatises were written.

The construction of pyramids was revived, albeit on a smaller scale (Lahun), while the largest temple of all time, mentioned by Herodotus in Book II of his History as the "labyrinth", was also built.

The 12th Dynasty drew to a close with the pharaoh Amenemhat IV and Queen Sebeknefru (1781 BC) and from this point the historical reconstruction becomes fragmentary and confused. There was a period of transition (the Second Intermediate Period) that, perhaps as a result of the weakness of the pharaohs of the 13th and 14th Dynasties, saw the gradual infiltration of the Nile delta by nomads of Semitic origin, perhaps arriving from Asiatic steppes. These people were called the Hyksos, a name deriving from the Grecian form of Heka-Kasutt (heads of foreign countries).

The capital of Egypt was moved to Avaris (Hat-Uart) in the Nile delta. The Hyksos domination of Egypt lasted around 250 years and spanned the 15th, 16th and 17th Dynasties which saw numerous successive pharaohs of

whom only a few names and rare works are known.

The Second Intermediate Period concluded around 1550 BC with the accession of Ahmose I, the progenitor of the 18th Dynasty during which Egypt was finally freed from foreign domination.

This period, the so-called "New Kingdom", saw great monarchs such as Queen Hatshepsut, Thutmosis III, one of the greatest Egyptian sovereigns and warriors and Amenhotep IV, better known as Akhenaten, the creator of the so-called "Amarna heresy" who introduced the cult of the solar disc Aten. Then came the boy-king Tutankhamun, famous for his tomb full of treasures.

The period of rebirth and prosperity continued into the 19th Dynasty (1291-1185 BC) with the reigns of great pharaohs who left testimony to their power in the form of monumental works: Sety I,

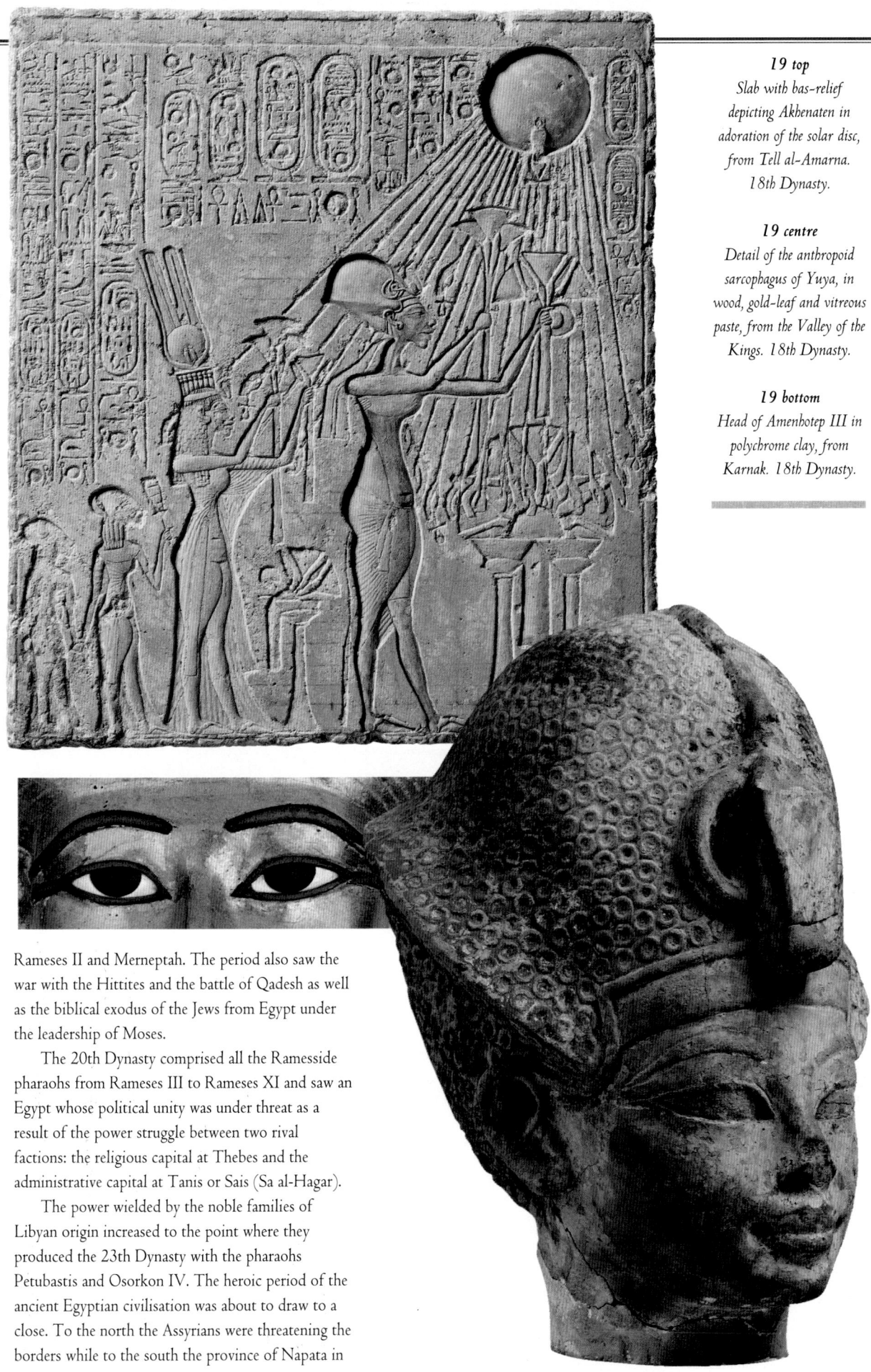

Rameses II and Merneptah. The period also saw the
war with the Hittites and the battle of Qadesh as well
as the biblical exodus of the Jews from Egypt under
the leadership of Moses.

The 20th Dynasty comprised all the Ramesside
pharaohs from Rameses III to Rameses XI and saw an
Egypt whose political unity was under threat as a
result of the power struggle between two rival
factions: the religious capital at Thebes and the
administrative capital at Tanis or Sais (Sa al-Hagar).

The power wielded by the noble families of
Libyan origin increased to the point where they
produced the 23th Dynasty with the pharaohs
Petubastis and Osorkon IV. The heroic period of the
ancient Egyptian civilisation was about to draw to a
close. To the north the Assyrians were threatening the
borders while to the south the province of Napata in

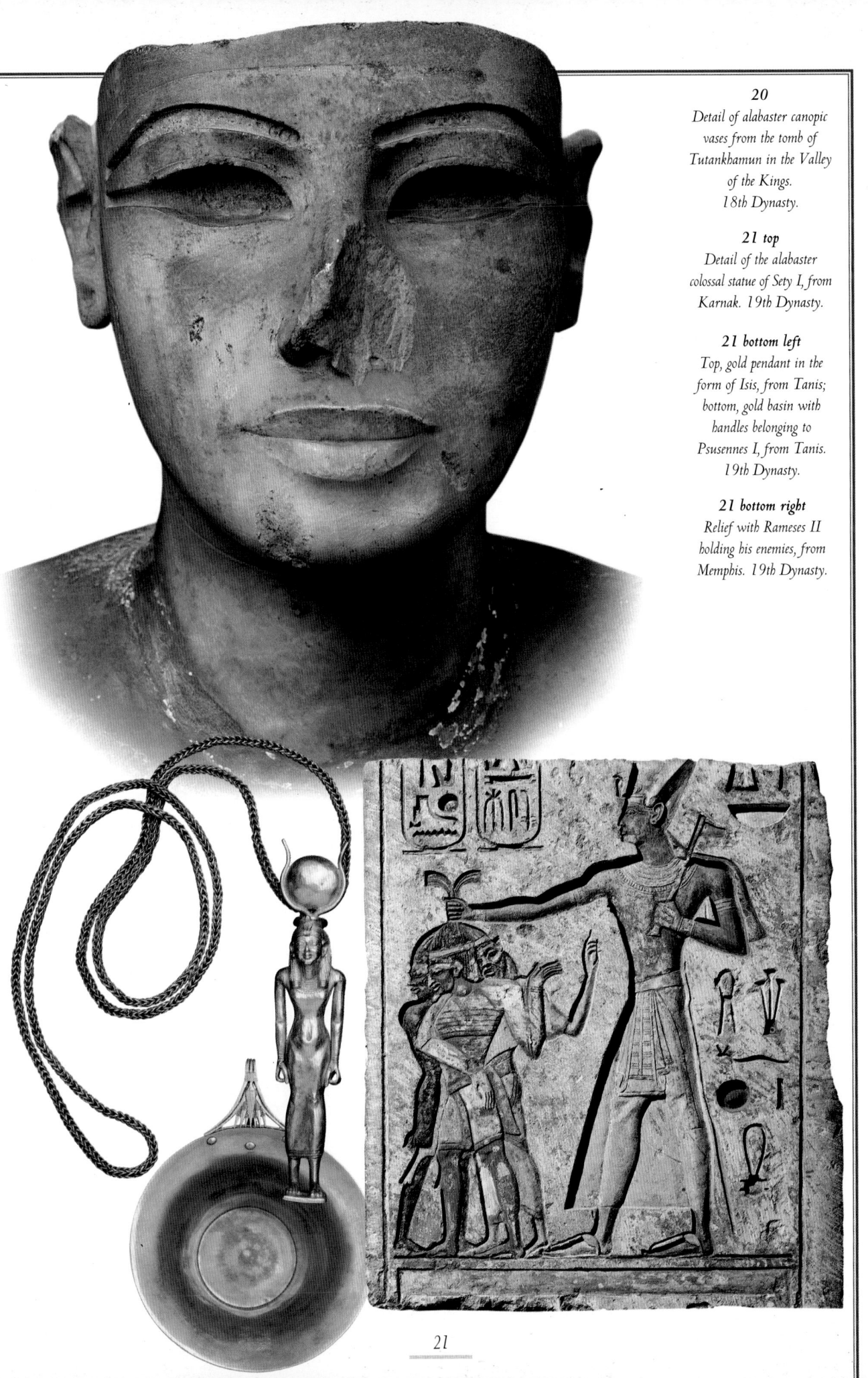

**20**
*Detail of alabaster canopic vases from the tomb of Tutankhamun in the Valley of the Kings. 18th Dynasty.*

**21 top**
*Detail of the alabaster colossal statue of Sety I, from Karnak. 19th Dynasty.*

**21 bottom left**
*Top, gold pendant in the form of Isis, from Tanis; bottom, gold basin with handles belonging to Psusennes I, from Tanis. 19th Dynasty.*

**21 bottom right**
*Relief with Rameses II holding his enemies, from Memphis. 19th Dynasty.*

upper Nubia rebelled and managed to gain independence; in 775 BC its rulers at Kush gave rise to the Kushite 25th Dynasty. The Assyrians penetrated Egypt in the first half of the VII century and exercised power through local vassals. There was one brief period of political and moral revival led by Psamtek I who succeeded in overthrowing the foreign domination and founding the 26th Dynasty (664-525 BC). This period saw a number of significant events such as the beginning of work on a canal linking the Red Sea and the Mediterranean, the development of iron working and possibly the circumnavigation of Africa. Sais was established as the new capital while the political structure was inspired by the Old and Middle Kingdom models. An overly-ambitious project of expansion towards the north-east led Egypt to catastrophe once again. Psamtek I's army was defeated initially by Nabucodonosor and definitively by Cambyses in 522 BC.

**22 left**
*Small alabaster head of
Alexander the Great, from
al-Yauta. Ptolemaic Period.*

**22 top right**
*Painted and gilded statuette
of a Ptolemaic queen, from
Karnak. Ptolemaic Period.*

The Persian dynasties reigned until 332 BC, when Alexander the Great defeated the Persian king Darius III. The Greek conquest marked the onset of the decline of the ancient culture and dragged the country into a new dimension dominated by a radically different school of thought.

On the premature death of Alexander in 323 BC, the government of Egypt was entrusted to Ptolemy, the son of Lagos, who in 304 BC became pharaoh with the name Ptolemy I Soter. Ptolemaic Egypt enjoyed another period of prosperity as the policies introduced led to social renewal and economic development, marked by notable architectural and artistic works such as the temples of Denera, Edfu, Kom Ombo, Esna and Philae. Many of these monuments have survived to the present day.

Alexandria became the centre of Greek culture in the Mediterranean, while Hellenism spread throughout the known world from the Egyptian port. The ancient Egyptian culture whose roots dated back millennia, nonetheless managed to keep its religious traditions alive. These traditions were combined with those of the Greeks, giving rise to new forms, partly because the ancient religion was always tolerated and respected by the conquerors. The pantheon of divinities was expanded and the artistic canons survived, albeit in a more modern, "revised" form. Alexandria itself was, however, already infused with the new Hellenist culture.

There were fifteen Ptolemaic pharaohs, including two women, Berenice IV and Cleopatra VII. The last of the line was Ptolemy XV, the son of Caesar and Cleopatra, perhaps better known as Caesarion. Following the suicide of Cleopatra and the execution of Caesarion by Octavian Augustus, Egypt became a province of the Roman empire. The Romans also greatly admired Egyptian culture and such was the emperors respect for the ancient traditions that they had themselves crowned and took the divine title of pharaoh.

The passion of Egyptian exoticism reached such a height that the worship of Isis and other esoteric cults was taken up in Rome and becàme particularly popular among the upper classes.

**22 bottom right**
*Stela of Ptolemy V in
painted and gilded
limestone, from Armant.
Ptolemaic Period.*

**23**
*Presumed portrait of
Cleopatra in white marble.
Ptolemaic Period.*

**25 top**
*Detail of the sarcophagus of
Yuya, from the Valley of the
Kings. 18th Dynasty.*

**25 bottom**
*Pictorial detail from the
tomb of Nefertari in the
Valley of the Queens.
19th Dynasty.*

**PREDYANSTIC PERIOD**
(4000 - 3000 BC)

Naqada I (4000 - 3500)
Naqada II (3500 - 3100)
**Dynasty 0 (circa 3000)**
Narmer

**PROTODYNASTIC PERIOD**
(2920 - 2575 BC)

**1st Dynasty (2920 - 2770)**
Aha (Menes ?)
Djer
Djet
Den
Adjib
Semerkhet
Qa'a
**2nd Dynasty (2770 - 2649)**
Hetepsekhemuy
Raneb
Nynetjer
Peribsen
Khasekhem
(Khasekhemwy)

**OLD KINGDOM**
(2649 - 2152 BC)

**3rd Dynasty (2649 - 2575)**
Sanakht 2649 - 2630
Djoser (Netjerkhet)
2630 - 2611
Sekhemkhet 2611 - 2603
Khaba 2603 - 2600
Huni 2600 - 2575
**4th Dynasty (2575 - 2465)**
Snefru 2575 - 2551
Khufu 2551 - 2528
Djedefra 2528 - 2520
Khafre 2520 - 2494
Menkaura 2494 - 2472
Shepseskaf 2472 - 2465
**5th Dynasty (2465 - 2323)**
Userkaf 2465 - 2458
Sahura 2458 - 2446
Neferirkara Kakai
2446 - 2426
Shepseskara 2426 - 2419
Neferefra 2419 - 2416
Nyuserra 2416 - 2392
Menkauhor 2392 - 2388
Djedkara Isesi
2388 - 2356
Unas 2356 - 2323
**6th Dynasty (2323 - 2152)**
Teti 2323 - 2291

Pepy I 2289 - 2255
Merenra 2255 - 2246
Pepy II 2246 - 2152

**FIRST INTERMEDIATE PERIOD**
(2152 - 2065 BC)

**7th Dynasty**
*A shadow dynasty. Manetho mentions "seventy kings of Memphis who ruled for seventy days" to indicate the period of confusion through which Egypt passed.*

**8th Dynasty (2152 - 2135)**
*About twenty ephemeral Memphite sovereigns are known. Qakara Aba, whose pyramid still stands at Saqqara, is the only king historically acknowledged.*
**9th and 10th Dynasties (2135 - 2040)**
*Dynasties in which the government of much of Egypt passed into the hands of the city of Hierankleopolis, before the Theban Dynasty got the power again.*
**11th Dynasty - first part (2135 - 2065)**
Mentuhotep I
Antef I
Antef II 2123 - 2073
Antef III 2073 - 2065

**MIDDLE KINGDOM**
(2065 - 1781 A.C.)
**11th Dynasty - second part (2065 - 1994)**
Mentuhotep II
Nebhepetra 2065 - 2014
Mentuhotep III
2014 - 2001
Mentuhotep IV
2001 - 1994
**12th Dynasty (1994 - 1781)**
Amenemhat I 1994 - 1964
Senusret I 1964 - 1929
Amenemhat II
1929 - 1898
Senusret II 1898 - 1881
Senusret III 1881 - 1842
Amenemhat III
1842 - 1794
Amenemhat IV
1793 - 1785
Queen Nefrusobek
1785 - 1781

**SECOND INTERMEDIATE PERIOD**
(1781 - 1550 BC)

**13th Dynasty (1781 - 1650)**
*Around seventy ephemeral sovereigns who reigned very shortly.*
**14th Dynasty (1710 - 1650)**
*An unknown number of ephemeral sovereigns all coeval to 13th and 14th Dynasties.*
**15th Dynasty (1650 - 1550)**
*Main Hyksos kings:*
Salitis
Sheshi
Jaqobher
Khayan
Apopi
Khamudi
**16th Dynasty (1650 - 1550)**
*Minor Hyksos governors ruling at the same time as the 15th Dynasty.*
**17th Dynasty (1650 - 1550)**
*Fifteen Theban sovereigns, the most important of whom are:*
Antef V
Sobekemsaef I
Sobekemsaef II
Antef VI
Antef VII
Seqenenra Tao I
Seqenenra Tao II
Kames

**NEW KINGDOM**
(1550 - 1075 BC)
**18th Dynasty (1550 - 1291)**
Ahmes 1550 - 1525
Amenhotep I 1525 - 1504
Thutmosis I 1504 - 1492
Thutmosis II 1492 - 1479
Hatshepsut 1479 - 1458
Thutmosis III 1479 - 1425
Amenhotep II
1424 - 1397
Thutmosis IV
1397 - 1387
Amenhotep III
1387 - 1350
Amenhotep IV/
Akhenaten 1350 - 1333
Smenkhkara
1335 - 1333
Tutankhamun
1333 - 1323

Ay 1323 - 1319
Horemheb 1319 - 1291
**19th Dynasty (1291 - 1185)**
Rameses I 1291 - 1289
Sety I 1289 - 1279
Rameses II 1279 - 1212
Merenptah 1212 - 1202
Amenemes 1202 - 1199
Sety II 1199 - 1193
Siptah 1193 - 1187
Tausret 1193 - 1185
**20th Dynasty (1187 - 1075)**
Sethnakht 1187 - 1184
Rameses III 1184 - 1153
Rameses IV 1153 - 1147
Rameses V 1147 - 1143
Rameses VI 1143 - 1135
Rameses VII 1135 - 1127
Rameses VIII 1127 - 1126
Rameses IX 1126 - 1108
Rameses X 1108 - 1104
Rameses XI 1104 - 1075

**THIRD INTERMEDIATE PERIOD**
(1075 - 664 CD)

**21th Dynasty (1075 - 945)**
Smendes I 1075 - 1049
Neferkara 1049 - 1043
Psusennes I 1045 - 994
Amenemope 994 - 985
Osorkon the Elder
985 - 979
Siamon 979 - 960
Psusennes II 960 - 945
**22th Dynasty (945 - 718)**
Sheshonq I 945 - 924
Osorkon I 924 - 899
Sheshonq II 890 circa
Takelot I 889 - 883
Osorkon II 883 - 850
Takelot II 853 - 827
Sheshonq III 827 - 775
Pimay 775 - 767
Sheshonq V 767 - 729
Osorkon IV 729 - 718
**23th Dynasty (820 - 718)**
Petubasty 820 - 795
Sheshonq IV 795 - 788
Osorkon III 788 - 760
Takelot III 765 - 756
Rudamun 752 - 718
**24th Dynasty (730 - 712)**
Tefnakht 730 - 718
Boccori 718 - 712
**25th Dynasty (775 - 653)**
Alara 775 - 765
Kashta 765 - 745

Piankhy 745 -713
Shabaqo 713 - 698
Shabataqo 698 - 690
Taharqo 690 - 664
Tanutamani 664 - 653

## LATE PERIOD
(664 - 332 BC)

**26th Dynasty (664 - 525)**
Psamtek I 664 - 610
Nekau 610 - 595
Psamtek II 595 - 589
Apries 589 - 570
Amasis 570 - 526
Psamtek III 526 - 525
**27th Dynasty (525 - 404)**
Cambyses 525 - 522
Darius I 521 - 486
Xerxes I 486 - 465
Artaxerxes I 465 - 424
Xerxes II 424
Darius II 423 - 405
Artaxerxes II 405 - 404
**28th Dynasty (404 - 399)**
Amirteus 404 - 399
**29th Dynasty (399 - 380)**
Nepherites I 399 - 393
Hakor 393 - 380
**30th Dynasty (380 - 342)**
Nectanebo I 380 - 362
Teos 362 - 360
Nectanebo II 360 - 342
**31th Dynasty (342 - 332)**
Artaxerxes III 342 - 338
Arse 338 - 336
Darius III 336 - 332

## HLLENISTIC PERIOD
(332 - 30 BC)

**The Macedonians (332 - 305)**
Alexander the Great
332 - 323
Philip Arrhidaeus
323 - 317
Alexander IV 317 - 305
**Ptolemaic Dynasty (305 - 30)**
Ptolemy I Soter
305 - 282
Ptolemy II Philadelphus
285 - 246
Ptolemy III Euergetes
246 - 222
Ptolemy IV Philopator
222 - 205
Ptolemy V Epiphanes
205 - 180

T. VI Philometor 180 - 164,
163 - 145
Ptolemy VII Neos
Philopator 145
P. VIII Euergetes
170 - 163, 145 - 116
P. IX Soter 116-110,
109-107, 88-80
P. X Alexander
110 - 109, 107 - 88
Ptolemy XI Alexander 80
P. XII Neos Dionysos
80 - 58, 55 - 51
Berenice IV 58 - 55
Cleopatra VII Philopator
51 - 30
Ptolemy XV Cesarion
36 - 30

## ROMAN PERIOD
(30 BC - 313 AD)
*Only the names of the emperors
mentioned in the hieroglyphic and demotic
texts are cited.*

Augustus 30 BC - 14 AD
Tiberius 14 - 37
Caligula 37 - 41
Claudius 41 - 54
Nero 54 - 68
Galba 68 - 69
Otho 69
Vespasian 69 - 79
Titus 79 - 81
Domitian 81 - 96
Nerva 96 - 98
Trajan 98 - 117
Hadrian 117 - 138
Antoninus Pius 138 - 161
Marcus Aurelius 161 - 180
Lucius Verus 161 - 169

Commodus 180 - 192
Septimus Severus 193 - 211
Caracalla 198 - 217
Geta 211 - 212
Macrinus 217 - 218
Diadumenianus 218
Alexandrer Severus 222 - 235
Gordian III 238 - 244
Philip 244 - 249
Decius 249 - 251
Gallus and Volusianus
251 - 252
Valerian 253 - 260
Gallienus 253 - 268
Macrianus and Quietus
260 - 261
Aurelian 270 - 275
Probus 276 - 282
Diocletian 284 - 305
Maximian 285 - 305
Galerius 293 - 311
Maximin Daia 305 - 313

# The Gods of Ancient Egypt

From the points of view of philosophy and history, the Egyptians conceived the world as the valley in which they lived, that is to say a land that developed vertically from north to south; a land that rises from the waters, just as out of the waters of Nun, the primordial ocean, were born the earth and the heavens. The other dominant element of this world that originated from water was the sun, the power of which was capable of baking the land and withering crops as well as bringing life, light and warmth.

Just as the waters of the Nile flowed northwards from the south, the earliest inhabitants of Egypt saw the sun rise and set on a trajectory from east to west that intersected that of the river. Each evening, the sun disappeared in the west as if had been swallowed by the sky, but during the night it was regenerated and appeared again the next day on the eastern horizon. From the earliest of times, the Egyptians used these simple natural observations to develop a vision of a world based on the terrestrial north-south and celestial east-west

axes which formed the foundation of their religious beliefs.

Curiously, as vital as the Nile was to their very existence, and despite the part it played in their vision of the world, the Egyptians never deified it, associating with divinities not the river itself but rather its effects. Thus, they identified Hapi, a god associated with the concept of abundance, with the phenomenon of the Nile flood, and similarly, the energy of the waters that revitalised and fertilised the land was associated with the resurrection myth of Osiris. Hence the correlation between the cult of the dead, the concept of divine resurrection and the fertilisation of the land that was probably developed as early as the Predynastic Period.

**26 top**
*Rameses II, depicted twice, prostrates himself before the solar disc. Drawing taken from Ippolito Rosellini's* Religious Monuments.

**26 bottom**
*The crocodile god, Sobek, in a drawing taken from Ippolito Rosellini's* Historical Monuments.

**26-27**
*Rameses II before Amun-Ra, Mut and the divine form of himself, from the Temple of Abu Simbel. Drawing taken from Ippolito Rosellini's* Historical Monuments.

**27 top**
*The god Ra-Harakhti, in a drawing taken from Ippolito Rosellini's* Historical Monuments.

**27 bottom**
*Sety I introduced by Horus before Osiris and Imentet. Drawing taken from Ippolito Rosellini's* Historical Monuments.

The Egyptians believed that the Nile flowed from a cavern, fed by the subterranean ocean of Nun, itself composed of the primordial waters from which the universe was created and on which the world floated. They thought that the great river flowed uninterruptedly towards the very waters that fed it and returned to the surface in an eternal and immutable cycle of regeneration. They also believed that the sun god Atum-Ra, creator of all things, rose out of the primordial ocean Nun; the sun in turn created two deities—Tefnut, the damp air and Shu, the dry air— who in their turn created the god Geb (the earth) and the goddess Nut (the sky). Out of the union of these last two came the gods Osiris, Isis, Seth and Nephthys. This conception of the world is a recurrent motif in

*28 left*
*Statue of the goddes Sekhmet, in gilded wood, found in the Tomb of Tutankhamun.*

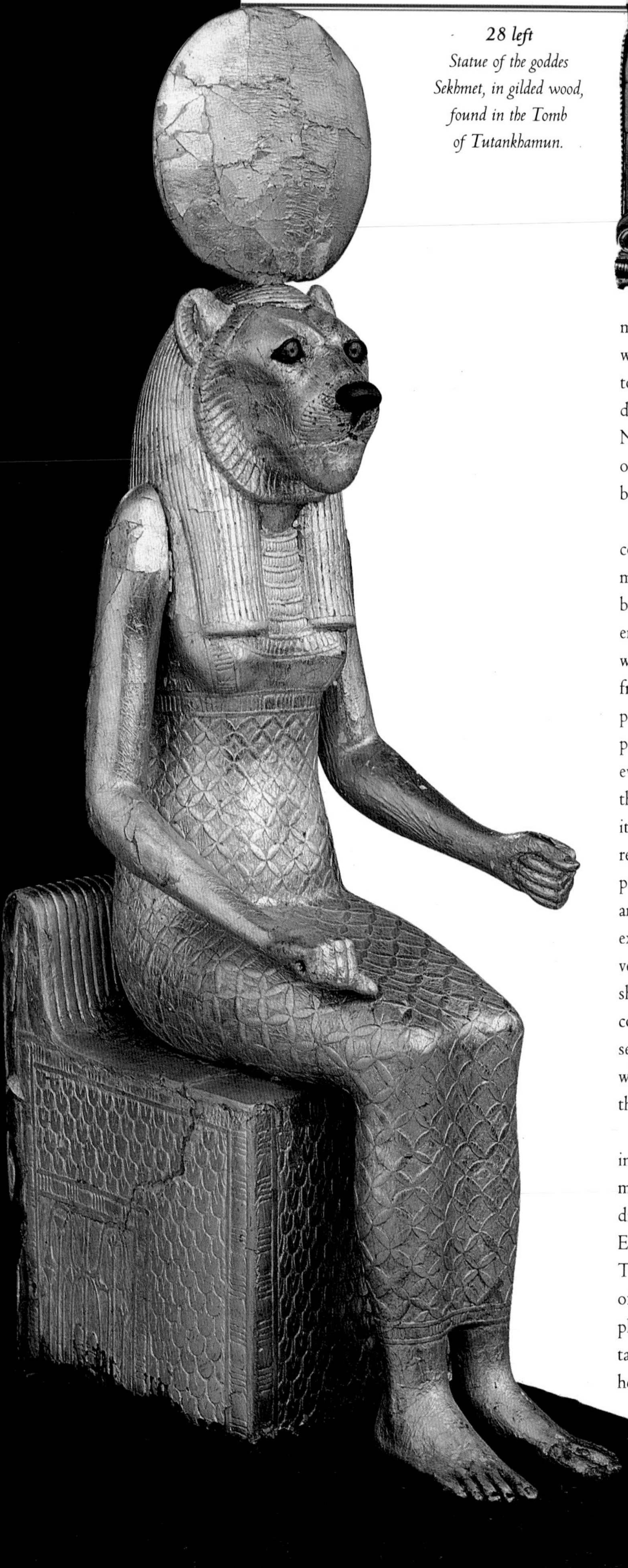

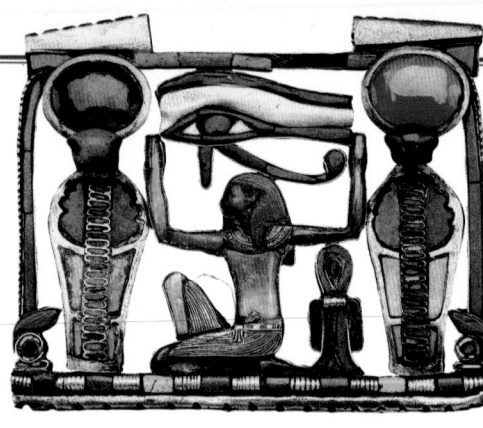

many images in which Nut is depicted as a naked woman, elongated and supported by the god Shu to prevent her from falling onto her consort Geb, depicted as a sleeping, naked man. Each evening, Nut swallowed the solar disc and gave birth to it once again in the morning; not infrequently, her body was depicted covered with stars.

The Egyptians' religious beliefs were very complex and their pantheon was populated by a multitude of different deities. In general, it may be said that ancient Egyptian culture in its entirety was permeated by religion: society itself was structured according to a rigidly hierarchy, from the gods to the pharaoh through to the people subdivided into classes. The gods personified the forces of nature, supervising every event and every activity; they were responsible for the destiny of the country and every inhabitant of it. The cults of the various gods were the responsibility of the pharaoh and the priests who provided for the terrestrial needs of each deity and the care of their material images according to extremely complex rituals. The people instead venerated their gods in small tabernacles and shrines constructed in the villages and the countryside. Moreover, each region, district and settlement had its own gods and its own myths which were accepted with absolute tolerance by the official clergy.

The minor deities (actually the most important in terms of popular religion) manifested themselves in multiple forms and took diverse names from place to place: the Egyptologists have identified several thousand. The Egyptian people had a practical conception of religion and associated every natural phenomenon with a particular deity who might take the form of animals, plants or natural events: hence the veneration of many animals such as cats, crocodiles and bulls which not infrequently were mummified and placed in

**28 right**
*Also part of the
Tutankhamun's funerary
goods, this necklace golden
counterpoise, with
semiprecious stones and
vitreous paste features some
figures representing eternity.*

special necropolises after their deaths. Among the gods worshipped throughout Egypt were Osiris, the Lord of the Underworld portrayed in the form of a mummy with a bluish flesh tone, his wife Isis, a witch and a powerful goddess of life and regeneration, the jackal-headed Anubis, the god of the necropolises and patron of mummification and Bes, depicted as a dwarf with monstrous features, the protector of pregnant women and god of the family.

Among the secondary deities most frequently encountered in Egyptian iconography are Maat, the goddess of justice, represented with a feather on her head, Khum, the god who modelled man on his potter's wheel, represented with a ram's head, Seth, the god of negativity and destruction, represented with the head of an unidentifiable animal, Hathor, the goddess of love, the arts and music, represented with the ears of a cow, Bastet, the beneficent goddess and protector of births, represented with the head of a cat, Thot, the god of writing and notary to the gods, represented with the head of an ibis, and Sobek, a god who protected the waters from enemies, represented with the head of a crocodile. Lastly, the deities venerated above all at Thebes, were the triad composed of Amun-Ra king of the gods and the solar deity, Mut, his wife, and Khonsu, their son and the god of the moon.

**29 foreground**
*Detail of a pectoral
depicting the goddess Nut,
in gold, cornelian and
vitreous paste. This jewel is
from the Tomb of
Tutankhamun, too.*

**29 background**
*This relief depicting the
goddess Isis with her wings
outspread decorates
Tutankhamun's inner
sarcophagus in solid gold.*

# The Cult of the Dead

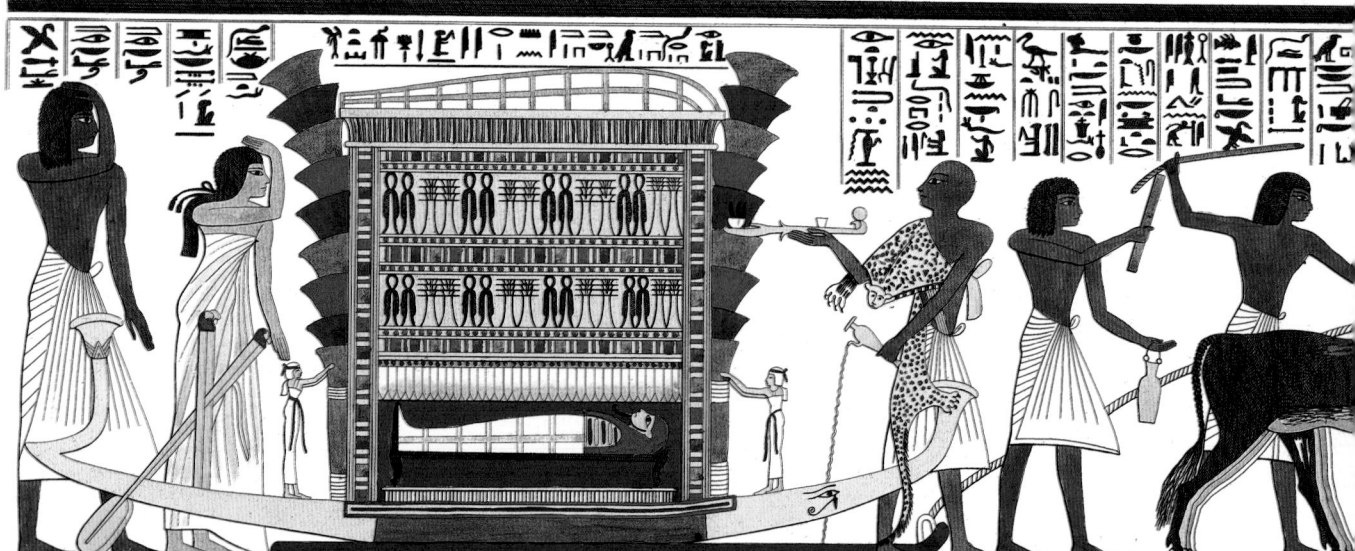

The evidence discovered by archaeologists demonstrates that ever since the Neolithic period, the inhabitants of Egypt had a profound belief in the existence of a spirit world in which the deceased would have needs similar to those they had known during their terrestrial existence.

It was actually in Egypt, in the first half of the 3rd millennium BC, at the time of the 3rd Dynasty, that the first true monumental tombs in history were built.

If in the Protodynastic Period, the royal tomb was already strictly connected to the affirmation of terrestrial power, by the time of the 3rd Dynasty, the tomb had also become a symbol of the pharaoh's divinity and of his power and celestial capacity to overcome death of which the whole country could benefit. To express these new concepts, Imhotep, Djoser's great chancellor and architect, designed the first stepped pyramid at Saqqara which symbolised a staircase towards the sky allowing the pharaoh's celestial ascension. This is an idea expressed on a number of occasions in the *Pyramid Texts*, collections of formulas and prayers that are found inscribed in the pyramids from the 5th Dynasty onwards and which subsequently evolved into the *Sarcophagus Texts* and the *Book of the Dead*.

*30-31*
*Funeral scenes from Theban tombs. Drawings taken from Ippolito Rosellini's* Civic Monuments.

**31 top**
*A Nile processional boat.
Drawing taken from
Ippolito Rosellini's*
Historical
Monuments.

**31 bottom**
*A funerary boat, from a
tomb at Beni Hassan.
Drawing taken from
Ippolito Rosellini's*
Historical Monuments.

Djoser's successors also adopted the concept of the pyramid-tomb which, during the reign of Snefru, the first pharaoh of the 4th Dynasty, acquired its definitive form as an expression of the ever greater importance attached to the solar cult in association with that of royalty. As the religious concept had evolved, the celestial staircase was no longer necessary: the steep sides of the pyramid, a manifestation in stone of the sun's rays, similarly allowed the pharaoh's spirit to reach the sky.

During the New Kingdom (1550-1075 BC), the Egyptian sovereigns, having abandoned the use of the pyramid form for royal tombs, had immense burial chambers dug into the rock and decorated with magical-religious texts; their contents would allow the deceased king to overcome the innumerable dangers that he would encounter on his journey through the underworld before joining the sun god Ra, of whom he was believed to be a son. Because the journey through the underworld was so perilous, the dead were accompanied by numerous amulets. Moreover, it was

thought that a particularly delicate phase existed between the moment of death and the true passage to the underworld, during which divine judgement, that not even the pharaoh could avoid, took place. The deceased, brought before the gods Osiris and Anubis, saw his own heart weighed by the god Thot on scales counterbalanced by a feather, the manifestation of Maat, the goddess of order and justice. If the two plates of the scales were balanced, then the deceased had been upright and honest during his terrestrial life and deserved to be welcomed by Osiris in the next world; otherwise, the spirit was devoured by a terrible monster and annihilated forever.

All of the New Kingdom's magnificent underground tombs contained fabulous funerary goods, as the tomb of Tutankhamun demonstrated. The funerary caches were considered to be crucial to making life in the underworld more pleasant and thus included everyday objects, furniture, games and foods of all kinds. Moreover, the tombs also contained special

**32 top**

*The god Anubis, intent on embalming a corpse. Wall painting from one of the Tombs of the Nobles.*

**32 centre**

*Four painted limestone vases carrying the name of Yuya and discovered in the Valley of the Kings. 18th Dynasty.*

**32 bottom**

*The "Tribune of Osiris" from the tomb of Rameses VI in the Valley of the Kings. Drawing taken from Ippolito Rosellini's* Religious Monuments.

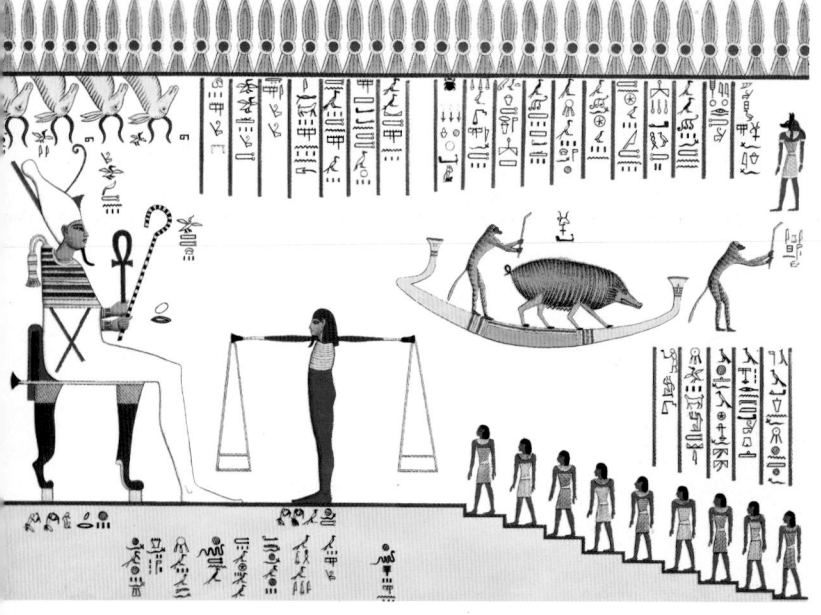

statuettes (*shwabty* figures) that, once brought to life in the underworld, would have obeyed the orders of the dead and completed the most onerous tasks in his place.

A large, richly appointed tomb was not the exclusive privilege of members of the royal family, but one also of high ranking dignitaries and even simple artists and craftsmen: they also prepared highly ornate tombs, although the decorative motifs were different to those of the royal tombs and were inspired by scenes of daily life rather than of the underworld.

The characteristic that differentiated the civilisation of ancient Egypt from all the others which developed in the Mediterranean basin and the Near East, was the perceived need to conserve the mortal remains of the deceased intact. As a consequence, embalming techniques were developed, initially in fairly rudimentary form in the 4th Dynasty, and became more elaborate during a process of evolution that reached its

height in the New Kingdom. Embalming continued to be practised in simplified forms in the Late Period and in the Graeco-Roman Period.

The funeral rituals were always very complicated. During the New Kingdom, following embalming, the coffin was transported by the deceased's relations to the west bank of the Nile on a boat adorned with flowers, amidst the laments of those present and the propitiatory prayers offered to Osiris and Anubis by the priests; the boat was followed by a fleet of other vessels carrying friends, furnishings and offerings. Having reached the west bank of the river (where the necropolises were located), the sarcophagus was placed on a wagon drawn by oxen and a funeral procession formed along the route to the tomb. Here the ceremony of the "opening of the mouth and of the eyes" was performed to allow the deceased to regain the ability to speak, see and feed himself in next world. The sarcophagus, the furnishings and the offerings were then placed in the tomb before it was sealed for all eternity.

*33*

*Detail of a wall painting in the burial chamber of the tomb of Tutankhamun in the Valley of the Kings. The scene depicts the ceremony of the opening of the mouth.*

# Hieroglyphic Writing

The deciphering of the hieroglyphs was the work of a young French scholar, Jean François Champollion, who in 1808 began to work on the so-called Rosetta Stone, the tri-lingual inscription in hieroglyphs, demotic and Greek characters, found in 1799 by the Napoleonic troops near the town of Rosetta in the Nile delta.

Born in 1790, Champollion soon devoted himself to linguistic and Oriental studies and his deep knowledge of numerous idioms, above all Coptic, was of great help to him in the study and unravelling of the secrets of hieroglyphic writing.

Appointed as a University of Grenoble professor at just nineteen years of age, Champollion devoted 14 years to the study of ancient Egyptian writing, basing his work on three remarkable intuitions: that the Coptic constituted the ultimate development of Egyptian, secondly that the hieroglyphs had a combined ideographic and phonetic meaning and, lastly, that the hieroglyphs enclosed within the cartouches transcribed phonetically the names of the pharaohs. Supposing that each hieroglyphic sign

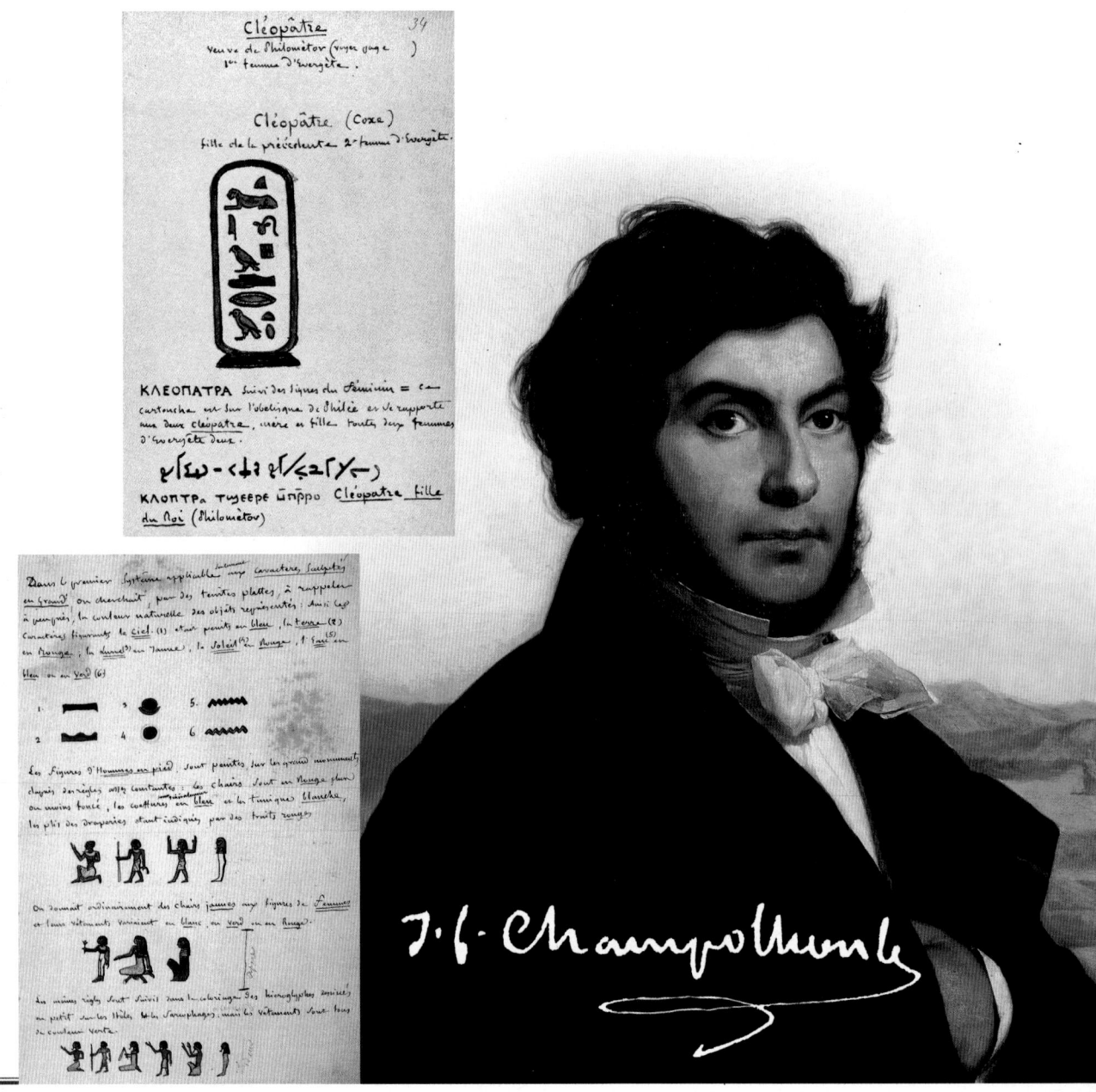

corresponded to a alphabetical sign and knowing
from the Greek text of the Rosetta Stone that the
king it referred to was Ptolemy, he managed to
identify the sings that formed the name PTOLMYS.

Later, in 1821, by analysing the bilingual text
(Greek and hieroglyphs), on an obelisk discovered
by Belzoni in the island of Philae and taken to
England, he managed to decipher the name of
Cleopatra and thus identify the alphabetical
equivalent of no less than 12 signs. Extending this
methodology to other cartouches, Champollion
discovered the equivalents of many hieroglyphs. In
1822 he presented his discovery to the academic
world in the celebrated *Lettre à M. Dacier*, the
secretary of the *Académie des Inscriptions et Belles Lettres*.

This was followed in 1824 by a book titled, *Précis
du système hiéroglyphique Egyptiens*, in which he explained
the fundamental concepts of hieroglyphic writing.
After having studied the inscriptions on numerous
relics conserved in the European collections,
Champollion, with the support of the king of
France, Charles X and the Grand duke Leopold II
of Tuscany, and accompanied by his most able
disciple, Ippolito Rosellini, organised the Franco-
Tuscan expedition that left Toulon for Egypt in
July, 1828. Having finally reached the land of the
pharaohs, Jean François Champollion was able to
confirm his discoveries in the field, giving voice
again to the language of ancient Egypt and founding
a new discipline, Egyptology.

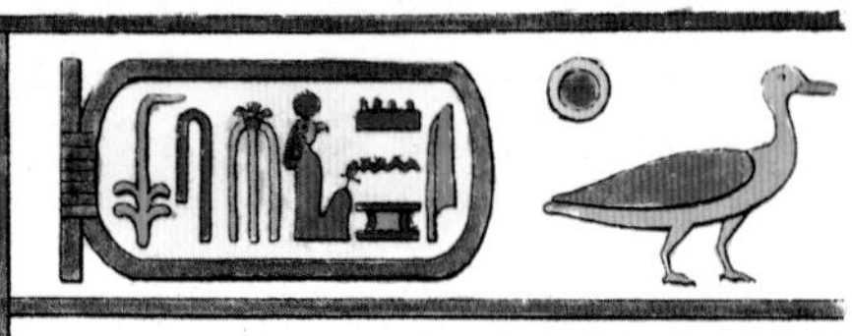

**36 top left**
*The god Thot, protector of the scribes. Drawing taken from Ippolito Rosellini's* Religious Monuments.

**36 top right**
*Cartouche with the name of the pharaoh, Horemheb, from his tomb in the Valley of the Kings.*

**36 bottom**
*Scribe's palette in ivory from the tomb of Tutankhamun.*

**37 top centre**
*Casket for brushes in gilded wood, part of the funerary cache of Tutankhamun.*

**37 left**
*Ivory papyrus burnisher, from the funerary cache of Tutankhamun.*

**37 top right**
*Scribe's palette in gilded wood, from the tomb of Tutankhamun.*

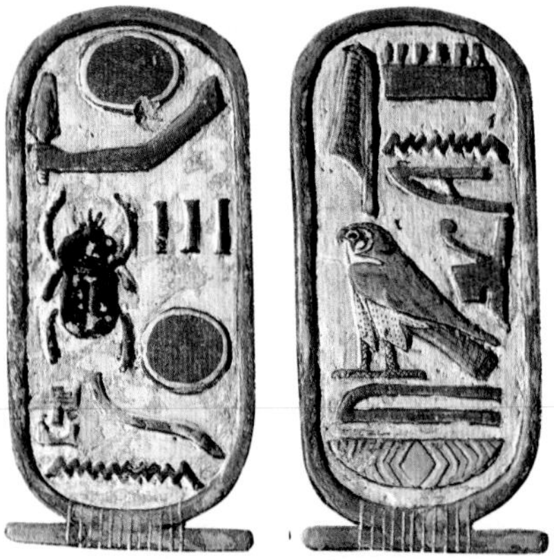

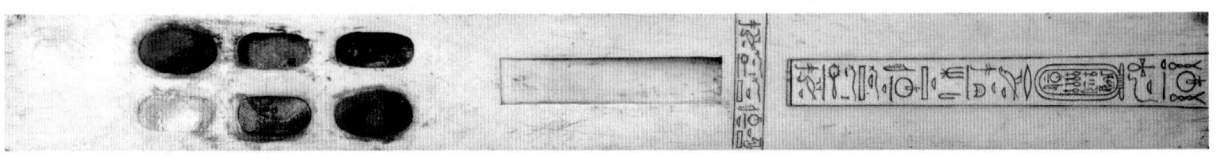

*37 bottom*
*Statue of a scribe in painted*
*limestone, from Saqqara.*
*5th Dynasty.*

# Travellers and Explorers

Following the publication of *Description de l'Egypte* and the writings of Champollion, there was a veritable race to Egypt on the part of academics, antiquarians, adventurers, traffickers, the merely curious and expert Egyptologists. Even in antiquity, travellers of greater or lesser fame had left traces of their passing; mention has to be made of Homer, Hecataeus of Mileteus, Herodotus, Diodorus Siculus, Strabo, Plutarch and Plinius.

The Roman emperors were by no means immune to the appeal of Egypt and many commissioned monuments such as the temple of Dendur by Octavian Augustus or the Trajan pavillion at Philae, or had their names inscribed on the existing monuments.

Then, for long centuries, Egypt and its monuments plunged into oblivion; travellers and merchants, in particular the Venetians, frequented the country through their trading links with the East, but never penetrated further into the country than Cairo. Only in 1589 did an unknown merchant, the so-called "Anonymous Venetian", ascend the Nile as far as Thebes and write the earliest account of a trip to Upper Egypt to have reached us.

**38 top**
Dominique Vivant Denon
(1747-1825), one of the
first Egyptologists, in an
early portrait.

**38 bottom left**
Egypt, as it appeared on a
map of the world drawn
between 1042 and 1072.

**38 bottom right**
The German Jesuit,
Atanasius Kircher (1602-
1680), the author of a
study of the correlation
between the Egyptian
calendar, the Gregorian
version and the Zodiac.

**38-39**
The measurement of the
Sphinx during the
Napoleonic expedition to
Egypt, in an illustration by
Vivant Denon.

**39 bottom**
Frontispiece of the
Déscription de
l'Egypte, in the edition
published by Pankoucke in
1825.

Other travellers were to visit the country sporadically over the next two centuries (including the German Jesuit Kircher, the Frenchmen Sicard, Volney and D'Anville and the Englishmen James Bruce and Henry Salt), but we have to wait for the great expedition led by Napoleon for the first true study of the monuments of Egypt supported by drawings and maps. In 1798, Dominique Vivant Denon and the scholars enrolled by Napoleon to accompany his army, explored Egypt, drawing, cataloguing and recording everything they found. The results of these labours were subsequently published in the *Déscription de l'Egypte*, a work of no less than nine volumes of text and eleven of folio-size plates, comprising three thousand drawings prepared by two hundred artists. The monuments of ancient Egypt, despite being covered with inscriptions, remained mute as far as the European travellers were concerned: in spite of the many attempts that were made, there was no way of deciphering the writings of the pharaohs. In 1799, when the Napoleonic adventure was drawing to a close, a certain Lieutenant Bouchard casually discovered near the town of Rosetta in the Nile delta, a stela that some years later was to prove to be the essential key to the hieroglyphs.

In the meantime, lots of discoveries were made: in 1813, the great Swiss orientalist, Johann Ludwig Burckhardt brought to

**40 top**
*The pasha Mohammed Ali, the undisputed ruler of Egypt from 1805 to 1849.*

**41 top left**
*Portrait in eastern barb of the traveller, Egyptologist and adventurer, Giovanni Battista Belzoni (1778-1823).*

**41 top right**
*The artist, traveller and diplomat, Henry Salt was appointed British consul general to Egypt in 1816.*

**40 bottom**
*Bernardino Drovetti (1776-1852), French consul, posing before a colossal head at Thebes in 1818.*

**41 centre**
*The recovery of a colossal bust of Rameses II at Thebes, directed by Belzoni in 1816.*

**41 bottom left**
*An enormous anthropoid sarcophagus, discovered by Heinrich von Minutoli in 1820.*

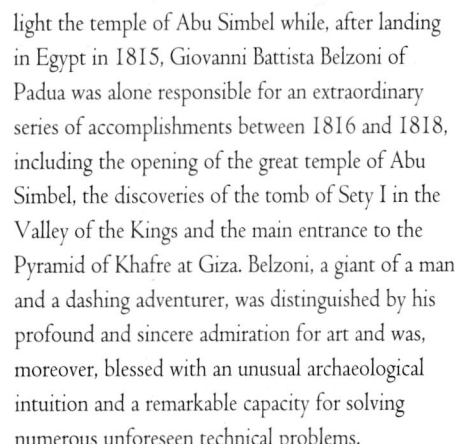

light the temple of Abu Simbel while, after landing in Egypt in 1815, Giovanni Battista Belzoni of Padua was alone responsible for an extraordinary series of accomplishments between 1816 and 1818, including the opening of the great temple of Abu Simbel, the discoveries of the tomb of Sety I in the Valley of the Kings and the main entrance to the Pyramid of Khafre at Giza. Belzoni, a giant of a man and a dashing adventurer, was distinguished by his profound and sincere admiration for art and was, moreover, blessed with an unusual archaeological intuition and a remarkable capacity for solving numerous unforeseen technical problems.

In 1820, another Italian, Girolamo Segato, discovered the entrance to the stepped pyramid of Djoser and mapped vast areas of Upper Egypt and Nubia, reaching as far as the distant Siwa oasis.

In 1828, a young French scholar, Jean François Champollion, of whom we have already spoken, together with his pupil Ippolito Rosselini, organised the Franco-Tuscan expedition to verify in the field the validity of his deductions and to tackle new epigraphic documents. It was out of Champollion's remarkable intuitions that the modern discipline of

**42 top left**
*The Pisan Egyptologist,
Ippolito Rosellini (1800-
1843), the author of* The
Monuments of Egypt
and Nubia.

**42 bottom left**
*Rameses II in the act of
massacring a number of
enemies of various races.
Drawing taken from
Ippolito Rosellini's*
Historical Monuments.

Egyptology was born. During his stay in the land of
the pharaohs, Rosellini not only co-ordinated the
execution of numerous epigraphic surveys and
drawings of the principal monuments of ancient
Egypt, but also acquired important archaeological
relics that now form the nucleus of the Egyptian
collection in Florence's Museum of Archaeology. On
his return to Italy he published, between 1832 and
1844, the material collected in his *Monumenti dell'Egitto e
della Nubia* (Monuments of Egypt and Nubia) from
which the illustrations on these pages are taken.

After his premature death, Champollion's work
was continued by the Prussian, Richard Lepsius who,
in 1842, organised an expedition which ascended the
Nile as far as Meroe. He returned to Germany in
1848 and subsequently published his fundamental
work, *Denkmäler aus Agypten und Athiopien*, dedicated to

**42-43**
*Rameses II aboard a war chariot, bas-relief in the hypostyle hall of the temple of Abu Simbel. Drawing taken from Ippolito Rosellini's* Historical Monuments.

**43 top right**
*right* Portrait of the Egyptologist Karl Richard Lepsius (1810-1884).

**43 bottom right**
*The great temple of Abu Simbel, reproduced in* Monuments of Egypt and Nubia, *published between 1849 and 1859 by Karl Richard Lepsius.*

the monuments of Egypt and Ethiopia.

Among the artists of the 19th century who depicted the splendours of the ancient kingdom of the pharaohs, mention is to be made of Emile Prisse d'Avennes and David Roberts. Prisse d'Avennes (1807-1879), an engineer and architect of French origin, arrived in Egypt in 1827 at the invitation of the pasha, Mohammed Ali. Blessed with an agile and brilliant intellect, along with a notable talent as a draughtsman, and driven by a great curiosity regarding the remains of the past, he soon began to study the pharaonic monuments, without ignoring the various examples of Islamic art present in the country.

In 1836, Prisse d'Avennes ascended the Nile as far as Abu Simbel and subsequently resided at Luxor; after leaving the Nile valley

**44**
*Rameses III from his tomb in the Valley of the Kings. Drawing by E.P. d'Avennes.*

**45 top left**
*The royal nurse holding the young Amenhotep II in her arms. By E.P. d'Avennes.*

**45 bottom left**
*A maid playing a lute in a bas-relief from the Theban tomb of Kenamun. Drawing by Emile Prisse d'Avennes.*

**45 top right**
*Portrait of the Egyptologist and adventurer, Emile Prisse d'Avennes (1807-1879), in eastern clothes.*

**45 bottom right**
*The representatives of some foreign peoples paying homage to Amenhotep IV. Sketch by Prisse d'Avennes.*

**46-47**
The great temple of Abu Simbel, with the colossal statues of Rameses II.

**46 bottom left**
The pronaos of the temple of Edfu, the second largest after that of Karnak.

**46 bottom right**
The Nile, in the vicinity of the fortress of Ibrim, today submerged by Lake Nasser.

The four lithographs reproduced here are taken from Egypt and Nubia (1846-1849), by David Roberts.

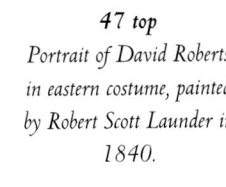

in 1844, he returned to France where he commenced publication of his drawings. Back in Egypt between 1858 and 1860, he devoted the rest of his life to the compilation of two works, the *Atlas de l'histoire de l'art égyptien* and *L'Art arabe d'apres le monuments du Caire*, the illustrations from which are still highly appreciated.

The Scotsman David Roberts (1796-1864), one of the most celebrated view painters of the 19th century, travelled to Egypt in 1838 and took the opportunity of depicting all the principal archaeological sites and the mosques of Cairo. The superb lithographs produced from his drawings, published for the first time in London between 1846 and 1849 under the title *Egypt and Nubia*, document the state of preservation of the Egyptian monuments in the 19th century and provide valuable evidence of the colours of many bas-reliefs which have today been almost completely lost. It should also be remembered that the documentary work performed by Roberts took on particular significance with regards to the Nubian temples that, following the construction of the great Aswan Dam, inaugurated on the 15th of January, 1971, had to be dismantled and rebuilt, frequently many kilometres away from their original sites. Moreover, many of the landscapes drawn by the artist have also been lost for ever.

# The Birth of Modern Archaeology

**48 top left**
Portrait of Gaston Maspéro (1846-1916), director of the Service des Antiquités Egyptiennes.

**48 bottom left**
A phase of Jacques de Morgan's recovery of the statues concealed in the "cachette" at Karnak in 1903.

**48 top centre**
Portrait of Auguste Mariette (1821-1881), creator of the Service des Antiquités Egyptiennes and founder of the Egyptian Museum of Cairo.

**48 right**
Portrait of the Egyptologist, Ernesto Schiaparelli (1856-1928), director of the Egyptian Museum of Turin.

**49**
The Valley of the Kings, November, 1922: Howard Carter and Arthur Callender open the doors of the four gilded wooden shrines containing the sarcophagi of Tutankhamun.

In 1850, a modest employee at the Louvre arrived in Egypt charged with the acquisition of Coptic manuscripts. This was Auguste Mariette. An acute observer and an expert on ancient texts, on his own initiative he organised digs at Memphis, between Saqqara and Abusir, thus bringing to light the Serapeum, the necropolis of the divine Apis bulls which were worshipped. This important archaeological discovery— to be followed by that of the lower temple of the Pyramid of Khafre—brought fame to the unknown clerk and in 1858 he was appointed by the Viceroy Said Pasha as conservator of monuments with extensive powers. He was responsible for the creation of the Museum of Cairo and, on his death in 1882, he was buried in the museum courtyard.

Mariette's successor was Gaston Maspèro who undertook important excavations at Giza and Luxor. He was also responsible for the discovery of the famous "cachette" of Deir al-Bahari where the mummies of a number of pharaohs from the 18th and 19th Dynasties were concealed (Amenhotep I, Rameses I and II and Sety I).

Between the end of the 19th and the beginning of the 20th centuries, archaeological campaigns followed one another in rapid succession, but were now regulated by legislation that required a fair division of

**50-51**
*Howard Carter
photographed while cleaning
the solid gold third coffin of
Tutankhamun.*

**50 bottom left**
*The treasure chamber, in the
tomb of Tutankhamun,
dominated by the fearsome
statue of Anubis.*

**50 bottom right**
*Arthur Mace and Alfred
Lucas, assistants to Howard
Carter, intent on the
restoration of one of the
guardian statues discovered
within the tomb of
Tutankhamun.*

the relics found between the countries financing the digs and the Egyptian government. Among the most well known financiers was the British aristocrat, George Edward Stanhope Molyneux Herbert, Earl of Carnarvon, who spent much time in Egypt for health reasons. Here Carnarvon met a young English archaeologist, Howard Carter (born in 1874), and commissioned him to undertake excavations on his behalf. After various digs, in 1914 Carnarvon obtained permission to work in the Valley of the Kings, an area that most experts considered to be archaeologically exhausted. On examining a number of clues, Carter was convinced that the valley contained an unknown tomb that ought to belong to the pharaoh Tutankhamun, a name that had been found on a stela discovered in the temple of Karnak and on a number of relics found in the valley itself. The outbreak of the First World War obliged Carter to postpone his search until 1917. Excavations went on with no great results till 1921. Lord Carnarvon, who had invested significant sums, was on the point of abandoning the enterprise and suspending his financial support, but allowed Carter to make one last attempt.

Work began in the autumn of 1922: on the 4th of November one of the workers found a stone step,

the first of a flight that descended into the rock. Carter, perhaps intuiting the long-awaited discovery, covered the find again and telegraphed Carnarvon in England, asking him to reach the site immediately. Work recommenced on the 24th of November and the staircase was soon cleared of detritus and the two Englishmen found themselves before a sealed doorway, followed by a second internal door. Both carried the seals of the necropolis and the name of Tutankhamun. On the 26th of November, Carter, Carnarvon and his daughter Evelyn, and the archaeologist Callender, who had recently joined the dig, could finally make a hole in the second door and observe the interior of the tomb and the treasures it contained. This was the first and to date, the only royal tomb to be found practically intact in the history of Egyptology, even though study of the remains revealed that in antiquity it had already been the object of two violations, fortunately without serious consequences.

The emptying of the tomb of Tutankhamun took years with around 3,500 objects being recovered, including the famous solid gold sarcophagus weighing over 110 kilograms, confirming that this was the most exceptional

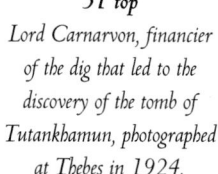

*51 top*
*Lord Carnarvon, financier of the dig that led to the discovery of the tomb of Tutankhamun, photographed at Thebes in 1924.*

*51 bottom*
*The antechamber of the tomb of Tutankhamun at the moment of discovery, with the pharaoh's dismantled war chariots and the ritual beds.*

archaeological find ever made in Egypt.

In 1939, the French archaeologist Pierre Montet, who was conducting a dig in the eastern region of the delta, at San al-Haggar, the site of the ancient city of Tanis, discovered the inviolate tombs of the pharaohs of the 21th and 22th Dynasties. The magnificent funerary cache found in the tomb of the pharaoh Psusennes, composed of jewels, gold and silver vases and gold masks, reveals remarkable artistry. Alongside the tomb of the sovereign, Montet discovered a further four belonging to Psusennes' successor, Amenemophis, the general Undjebaunded, Osorkon II and the pharaoh Sheshonq II. The discovery of the royal necropolis of Tanis and its treasures closed an era in the history of Egyptology which had begun with the discoveries of Belzoni and continued with that of Carter. However, Egypt has continued to reserve surprises for the researchers: finds of great importance have in fact continued up to the present day.

In 1989 an extremely interesting cachette (a hiding place) was found within the Temple of Luxor that contained statues in perfect condition and dating from the New Kingdom. They can today be seen in the Museum of Luxor's new gallery. The discovery that has aroused most interest around the world has been, however, that of a necropolis from the Roman Period, between the 1st and 2nd centuries AD, in the Bahariyya

oasis; in 1996, a donkey's hoof sank into the sand and the small hole produced revealed the existence of a subterranean tomb. In the months that followed, the excavations directed by the celebrated Egyptian archaeologist Zahi Hawass brought to light around a hundred mummies wrapped in gilded cartonnage; for this reason the necropolis is now known as the "Valley of the Golden Mummies". As the area is very extensive, the exerts believe that in the future over 10,000 may be found and that the excavation work could last for decades. Another very recent discovery is that of the intact tomb of the plenipotentiary governor of the Bahariyya oasis who lived during 26th Dynasty (around 500 BC, prior to the conquest of Egypt by the Persian Cambyses) when the oasis was at the height of its economic development. The tomb was found to contain a limestone sarcophagus with hieroglyphic inscriptions and a cache comprising amulets in gold and faience. Lastly, at Alexandria, the Frenchman, Frank Goddio, an expert in submarine archaeology, has brought to light numerous relics and identified the submerged island of Antirrodos where Cleopatra had a palace.

**53 top**
The famous Egyptian archaeologist, Zahi Hawass cleaning some of the mummies

from the oasis of Bahariyya. This location has become famous as the "Valley of the Golden Mummies".

**53 bottom**
In 1995, in the waters off the port of Alexandria, a team led by the French

archaeologist, Frank Goddio, discovered numerous monumental remains, statues and sculptural

fragments, perhaps belonging to one of Queen Cleopatra's palaces and the celebrated Lighthouse.

**54**
*In this bas-relief from the temple of Edfu, the goddesses Nekhbet and Uaget are placing the double crown of Upper and Lower Egypt on the head of the pharaoh.*

**55**
*The pronaos of the temple of Edfu is preceded by this celebrated granite statue of the god Horus in the form of a falcon with its head bearing the double crown.*

# *Archeological Itineraries*

# Alexandria

Known in Arabic as Al-Iskandariya, Alexandria is situated in the extreme north of Egypt, on the strip of land separating the Mediterranean from Lake Mariyut. It was founded by Alexander the Great in 332-331 BC, on the site of the Egyptian town of Rhakotis. The great Macedonian conqueror intended to provide Egypt with a new capital and Mediterranean Greece and the East with a port, preferring this option to the destroyed Tyre due to its more central position which made it a potential centre of trade in the Mediterranean. It is not known whether Alexander intended the city to be one of the metropolises of the universal empire he dreamed of, but the site soon proved to be well chosen. However, he did not stay there long enough to see a single building completed.

Following his mysterious visit to the priest of the temple of Jupiter-Amun in the Siwa oasis, Alexander departed to devote himself to the conquest of Asia. Eight years later, he died prematurely at 33 years of age. His body was embalmed and placed in a tomb in Alexandria with all the honours and funerary rituals normally accorded to a pharaoh.

One of Alexander the Great's generals, Ptolemy, promptly took up the reins of power and installed a new dynasty destined to endure for around three centuries until Cleopatra VII's suicide in 30 BC.

Under the aegis of the Ptolemaic Dynasty, Alexandria became a flourishing, cosmopolitan city, the largest in the ancient world before Rome imposed its supremacy, thanks to extensive trading with the peoples of the Mediterranean. The union of the Greek and Egyptian cultures meant that to all intents and purposes the city also became the cultural centre of the country. Thanks to thinkers and scientists such as Euclid, Aristarchus of Samos, Eratosthenes, Herophilus and Eratistratus, it was also the cradle of methodological criticism and philology, classical geometry and astronomy, map-making, the medicine of the central nervous system and the circulation of blood. Classical literature mentions two extraordinary institutions of learning and scientific research, the Library and the Museum. Unfortunately nothing now remains of either, and nor of the Pharos lighthouse, considered to be one of the Seven Wonders of the World. A

*56 top*
*The fortress of Qaitbey, erected in the 15th century on the foundations of the famous lighthouse of Alexandria.*

*56 bottom left*
*A view of the Museum of Graeco-Roman Antiquities which conserves remains from the period 300 BC to 300 AD.*

*56 bottom right*
*A detail of a sandstone lion conserved in the Museum of Graeco-Roman Antiquities.*

**57 bottom right**
*This elegant Hathoric capital is also part of the Museum of Graeco-Roman Antiquities collection.*

visit to the modern city of Alexandria will hardly satisfy a tourist interested in antiquities. Echoes of the past can be heard, it is true; you will be aware of being in the vicinity of the tomb of Alexander the Great or the palace of Queen Cleopatra but this has all now vanished forever. All that remain are the Temple of Serapis and the large Caesareum temple, probably begun by Cleopatra and completed during the reign of Augustus. You may also observe remains of the Roman baths and the so-called "Pompey's Column". Of more interest is a visit to the ancient catacombs, the most important of which are those of Komesh-Shuqafah, dating from the 2nd century AD. Lastly, various works of sculpture and painting and several mosaics are conserved in the local Graeco-Roman museum.

**57 left**
*The so-called Pompey's Pillar, no less than 27 metres tall and faced by a sphinx, was in reality erected by Diocletian in 292 AD.*

**57 top right**
*The Museum of Graeco-Roman Antiquities contains prevalently local relics.*

# Tanis

**58 top and centre**
*Among the remains of the Great Temple of Tanis, of particular note are the fragments of two sandstone colossal statues of Rameses II.*

**58 bottom**
*The tip of one of the obelisks that adorned the Great Temple of Amun.*

Tanis (Za'net in Egyptian), the capital of the 14th Nome of Lower Egypt is situated on the eastern side of the Nile delta, around 130 kilometres north-east of Cairo and 50 from the Mediterranean. The first survey of the site was made by the Napoleonic expedition, while the Frenchman Rifaud completed the first systematic excavations in 1825 and found the two large, pink granite sphinxes now conserved in the Louvre. Since then, archaeological work has continued almost uninterruptedly, directed by eminent Egyptologists such as Mariette, Petrie, P. Montet and J. Yoyotte. These excavations have mainly brought to light relics datable from the 21th Dynasty through to the Ptolemaic Period.

The casual discovery of relics from the Ramesside epoch and earlier periods prompted suggestions that this may have been the biblical city of Pi-Rameses, built by the Jews and their point of departure towards the promised land. The enigma has in part been resolved. It now appears certain that the stones of earlier times were transported to the sites in question for successive rebuilding work, a common practice among the ancient Egyptians. The site's principal feature is the reamins of the great temple of Amun, protected by a rectangular enclosure wall of brick measuring 430 x 370 metres within which — and in part integral with — is a second, the bricks of which are inscribed with the name of the pharaoh Psusennes I of the 21th dynasty.

At the centre of the enclosure stood the great Temple of Amun, now reduced to an expanse of columns, obelisks and statues of different eras with inscriptions and decorative motifs generally dating back to Rameses II. To the north of the temple is a sacred lake while to the east are the ruins of a granite temple. The Temple of Mut and Khonsus, also known as the Temple of Anta stands outside the brick curtain walls.

In 1866, the German Egyptologist, Karl

*58-59*
*A statuary group and a colossus statue of Rameses II stand in front of the temple pylon.*

*59 bottom*
*The entire Tanis archaeological area is studded with decorated blocks of granite, architectural fragments and monumental remains belonging to diverse temple complexes.*

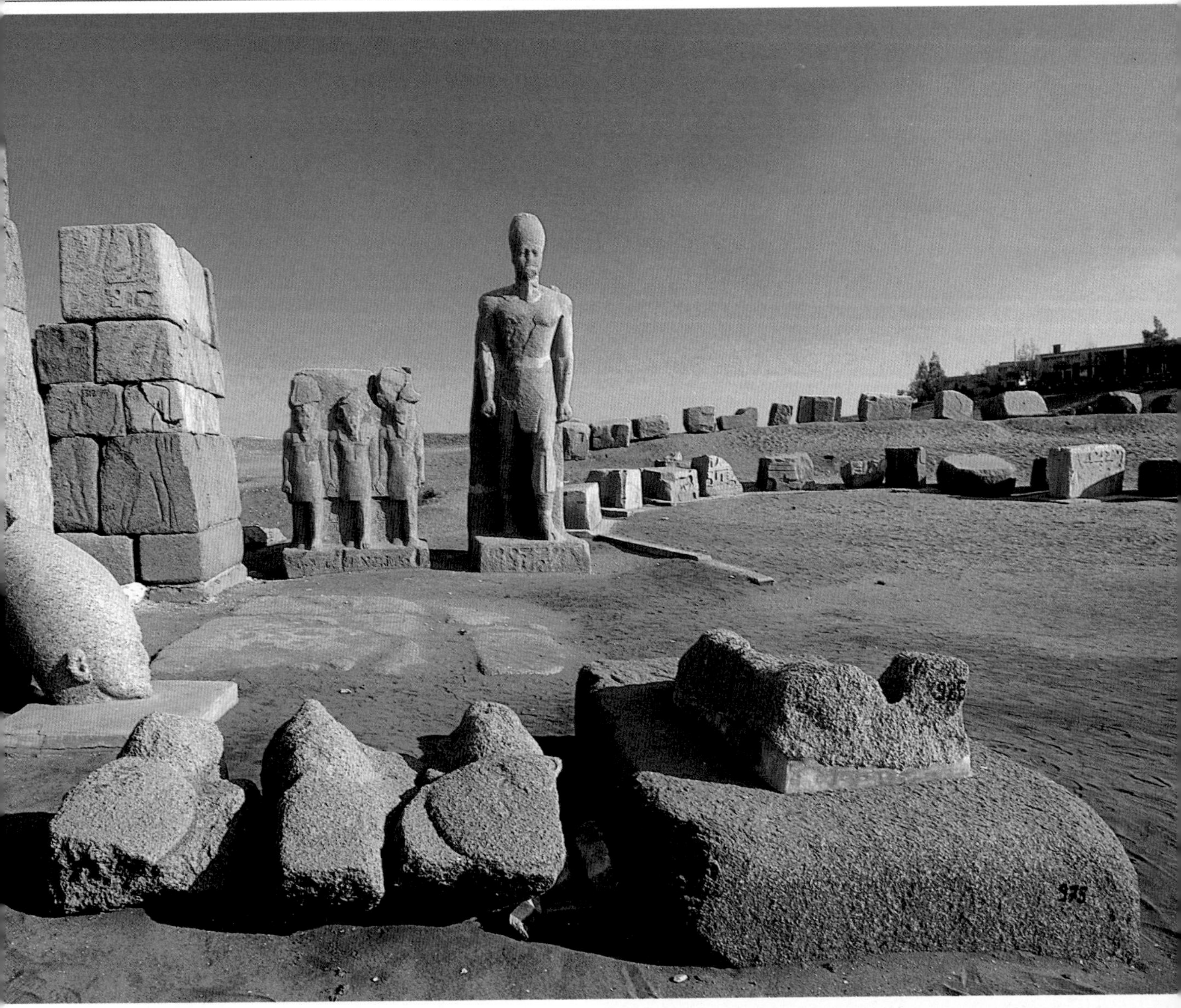

Lepsius, discovered a block of stone at Tanis that has become known as the Canopus Decree (comparable in importance to Egyptology to the Rosetta stone). On one side it carries a hieroglyphic inscription and its Greek translation, and one the other the same text in demotic characters.

In 1939, the French Egyptologist, Montet, made a discovery second in importance only to that of the tomb of Tutankhamun: a subterranean necropolis with the intact royal tombs of Psusennes I, Osorkon II and Sheshonq III (21-22 Dynasties). The precious finds, silver sarcophaghi, gold masks and jewels are now exhibited in the Egyptian Museum of Cairo.

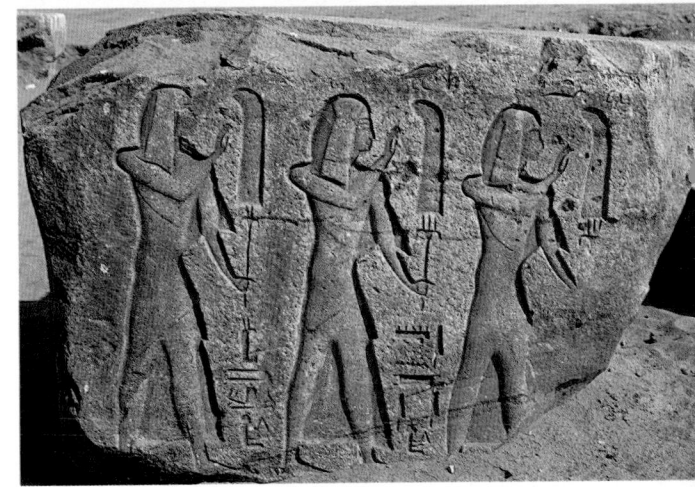

**60 left**
*The solid gold funerary mask of Psusennes I, discovered at Tanis by Pierre Montet.*

**60 bottom right**
*Gold and lapis lazuli pectoral of Sheshonq II, found at Tanis.*

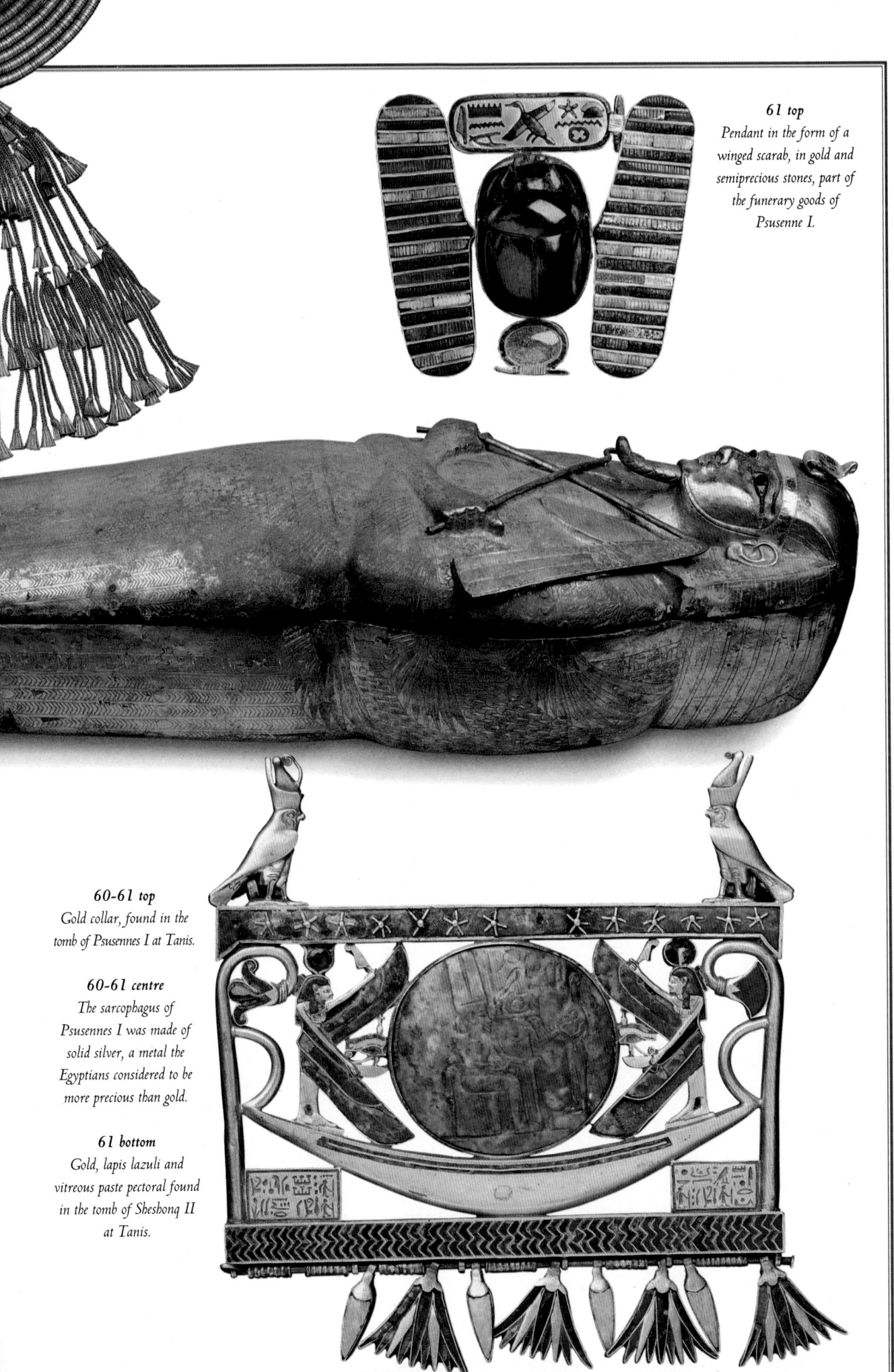

**61 top**
*Pendant in the form of a winged scarab, in gold and semiprecious stones, part of the funerary goods of Psusenne I.*

**60-61 top**
*Gold collar, found in the tomb of Psusennes I at Tanis.*

**60-61 centre**
*The sarcophagus of Psusennes I was made of solid silver, a metal the Egyptians considered to be more precious than gold.*

**61 bottom**
*Gold, lapis lazuli and vitreous paste pectoral found in the tomb of Sheshonq II at Tanis.*

# —Giza's Plateau—

Located around 12 kilometres from Cairo, the Giza Plateau extends on the edge of the Western Desert. The flat, regular conformation of the plateau made it an ideal site for the construction of monuments, while its position to the west of the Nile, that is to say, towards the setting sun, was a religious prerequisite for necropolises. The vicinity of the river also facilitated the transportation of materials.

A bed of nummulite fossils (foraminiferous protozoa common in the warm seas following the Jurassic, around 100,000,000 years ago) dating from the late Cretaceous, early Tertiary period has been discovered to the north-west of the plateau.

The slope extends towards the south-east with alternate strata of hard and soft rock: in this area the ancient Egyptians removed the softer limestone to reach the harder strata which they cut up into blocks to use for the construction of pyramids, tombs and temples.

Towards the south rises an irregular relief feature (Maadi) characterised by numerous chasms, wadis (dry river beds) and gorges from which the stones and clay needed for building were extracted.

These were materials of good quality, easily extracted and close to the building sites.

The white limestone used for the outer covering of the pyramids came from Tura, on the east bank of the Nile, whilst the granite arrived by river from Aswan (as testified by the bas-reliefs in the 5th Dynasty pyramid of Unas in nearby Saqqara).

What is perhaps the oldest tomb on the plateau was discovered by an Italian, Barsanti, in 1904, around 5 kilometres from the pyramid of Khufu, while a little higher is a mastaba from the 2nd Dynasty. Already considered to sacred before the construction of the great pyramids, this area was called Kheret-Neter-Akhet-Khufu (Necropolis of the horizon of Khufu). It was also known as Rostaw, a reference to the legend whereby Osiris was the god of the dead and "Lord of Rostaw"; that is to say, the sovereign of the caverns and passages thought to lie beneath the Giza plateau. In the light of recent excavations conducted by Zahi Hawass, the existence of such passages is more plausible today.

The plateau is, of course dominated by the three great pyramids and the Sphinx.

*62-63*

*A panoramic view of the archaeological area of Giza: in the foreground rises the Pyramid of Menkaura.*

# THE PYRAMIDS

## THE PYRAMID OF KHUFU

Built during the reign of Khufu between 2551 and 2528 BC, the Great Pyramid was almost certainly conceived as a funerary monument for the pharaoh's burial; little is known about Khufu's era and many hypotheses regarding the monument should be treated with caution.

Herodotus recounts that the pyramid was built over the course of 20 years, with 100,000 men working three-monthly shifts; statistics which might not be far from reality. The pyramid form had a religious-symbolic significance associated with the representation in stone of solar rays or the primordial hill at the origins of the world.

Considered by the ancients to be one of the Seven Wonders of the World, the building still arouses admiration and awe, due both to its sheer bulk and the surprising precision of its dimensions given the instruments available 4,500 years ago.

The sides of the base measure 230.40 x 230.51 x 230.60 x 230.54 metres, the total difference of just 20 cm equating to a margin of error of one in a thousand. At 146.59 metres in height, the Great Pyramid was the world's tallest building until the construction of the Eiffel Tower in 1889. The volume of around 2,700,000 cubic metres is composed of around 2,500,000 blocks of stone weighing on average 2,500 kg each.

The precision of the geographical alignment of the entrance face is equally surprising. The deviation from due north is just 0° 3' 6".

The present-day stepped appearance is due to the removal, during the period of Arab domination, of the external covering in white Tura limestone which would have made the pyramid glow brightly in the sun.

Today the summit is truncated, creating a platform, but in the past it would have terminated at 146.59 metres with a possibly gilded *pyramidion*. The entrance is situated on the north face at a height of about 15 metres. The current access, a passage created by ancient tomb robbers is lower. A descending corridor leads to a subterranean chamber, while a rising passage instead leads to the Grand Gallery and the Queen's Chamber. The latter was not actually a female royal tomb, but was named as such by the Arab visitors due to its unusual double pitched ceiling.

The King's Chamber, the object of controversy and unresolved mystery, features walls dressed with monolithic blocks of granite, the same material also being used for the 9 ceiling slabs. All of the granite elements are perfectly hewn and fit together with absolute precision. The monolithic sarcophagus, made of the same type of pink granite, lacks and inscriptions and the cover is missing.

Outside the building, alongside the east face, are three satellite pyramids attributed to the queens Hetepheres, Meritetes and Henutsen; on the south side of the pyramid, the Museum of the Solar Boat contains a perfectly restored and reassembled funerary boat over 40 metres long that would once have sailed on the Nile.

**66-67**
*A view of the Pyramid of Khafre which reveals the limestone covering of the summit.*

**66 bottom left**
*The Pyramid of Khafre throws its shadow on that of Khufu, surrounded by the vast necropolis.*

## THE PYRAMID OF KHAFRE

While smaller that the Pyramid of Khufu (215 x 215 x 143.5 m), the Pyramid of Khafre is nonetheless impressive as it is situated slightly higher than the other and its external covering has survived at the top below the tip.

The entrance is located on the north side and was discovered by Giovanni Belzoni in 1818; at the end of a long corridor is a single funerary chamber, excavated in the rock and featuring a ceiling of limestone slabs. A black granite sarcophagus with no inscriptions stands in the chamber.

## THE PYRAMID OF MENKAURA

This is the smallest of the three (102.2 x 104.6 x 65 m), but must have extremely beautiful as it was once coated with pink granite.

The entrance is located at the base of the north side and leads, by way of a corridor, to a unfinished mortuary chamber excavated in the rock at a depth of around 6 metres. A second passage leads to the burial chamber. Here a basalt sarcophagus was discovered, lacking inscriptions but decorated with architectural motifs. Unfortunately the relic was lost in a shipwreck while being transported to Europe.

**66 bottom right**
*A view of the Pyramid of Menkaura, with the three satellite pyramids.*

**67 top**
*Another view of the Pyramid of Khafre.*

**67 bottom**
*The tomb of Seshmnefer, a court dignitary from the late 4th Dynasty.*

**68 top**
*The Sphinx is no less than
20 metres high: the head
alone measures around
5 metres.*

**68 bottom**
*This view allows
the size of the monument,
57 metres long,
to be appreciated.*

## THE SPHINX

The Sphinx is located around 500 metres east of the Pyramid of Khafre, along the monumental road that linked the funerary temple with the lower temple of the pharaoh. The monument was sculpted in the living limestone of the plateau, utilising a protuberance in the terrain that was probably created by quarrying work.

The human head is wearing a *nemes* headcloth with an asp and the false beard of the pharaohs (relics found in the sand by G. Caviglia), while the body is that of a crouching lion, a symbol of regal power. The face of the pharaoh is thought to be that of Khafre himself.

Between the front paws stands the stela of Thutmosis IV, commemorating a premonitory dream of the pharaoh according to which he would have acceded to power had he brought to light the sphinx which had on a number of occasions been buried by the sand. That scrupulous observer Herodotus, perhaps did not mention the Sphinx because he could not actually see it. The ruins of the temple on which the sphinx rises (the Temple of the Sphinx) flank the Lower Temple of Khafre, the architecture of which features incredibly precise masonry with large granite blocks being used for columns, architraves and internal coverings.

While on the Giza plateau you should also visit the (where accessible) 4th and 5th Dynasty mastabas around the Pyramid of Khufu.

*68-69*

*The construction of the Sphinx is attributed to Khafre, the pharaoh whose facial features the colossus is thought to represent.*

# — The Egyptian Museum in Cairo —

**70 top**
*Sphinx of Thutmosis III located outside the museum.*

**70 top centre**
*An unusual view of the hall of the Egyptian Museum.*

**70 bottom centre**
*One wing of the museum's Honour Gallery.*

**70 bottom**
*The summit of an obelisk of Rameses II, from Tanis, now located in the garden of the museum.*

Those approaching the art and culture of ancient Egypt for the first time are faced with such a vast quantity of material that it is almost impossible to gain a complete overview. Visiting the Egyptian Museum in Cairo is thus indispensable for placing in context such a variety and abundance of archaeological marvels and for tracing a more exhaustive picture of what the Egyptians were capable of from the dawn of the Bronze Age, around 4,500 years ago.

Created in 1858 by the Frenchman Auguste Mariette, in river port buildings in the Bulaq quarter, the first collection of Egyptian antiquities was moved in 1902, to its present location close to the Midan al-Tahrir square, almost on the Nile banks. The building has not been subjected to significant modifications, something which cannot be said of the chaotic urban context in which it is set: besieged by the city, the present-day museum is immersed in gardens containing dozens of sculptural works and the mausoleum of its founder who was reluctant to be separated from the magnificent collections even after his death.

The museum's over 100 rooms contain the world's largest collection of Egyptian antiquities, around 100,000 works, while the stores also contain tens of thousands of relics.

The two-tier exhibition criteria were established by Mariette himself: the ground floor is devoted to the great sculptural works, arranged chronologically, covering the history of Egypt from the Archaic and Protodynastic Periods through to the Late, Saitic, Persian and Graeco-Roman Periods. The first floor instead features collections subdivided according to types of objects.

Visitors enter the Great Gallery on the ground floor which houses the stone sarcophagi of the Old Kingdom, and then encounter the statues of the great sovereigns from the era of the pyramids, between the 3rd and the 4th Dynasties (from the limestone simulacrum of Djoser to the

**70-71**

*The facade of the Egyptian Museum, overlooking a garden adorned with relics*

*from throughout Egypt. Building work on the museum began in 1897 and it was opened in 1902.*

**71 bottom left**

*A statue of a seated lion in pink granite, dating from the Late Period and discovered at Tell al-Muqdam. This piece is also located in the museum garden.*

**71 bottom right**

*The wide central room of the Egyptian Museum, surrounded by the other rooms where finds are displayed.*

diorite statue of Khafre and the triads of Menkaura, in polished schist), and high ranking figures such as the polychrome sculptural group of the priest Rahotep, son of the 4th Dynasty king, Snefru, and his wife Nefret, found at Meidum.

Gravitating around the colossal statue of Amenhotep III sitting alongside his wife Tiy that occupies the central corridor and proceeding in a clockwise direction through the ground floor rooms one finds statues and stelae relating to the sovereigns of the Middle Kingdom (Amememhat III and Senusret I), the New Kingdom (from the statue of Thutmosis III as a boy, to the sphinx with the features of Queen Hatshepsut, up to the four colossal statues of the heretical pharaoh Akhenaten, absolutely unique with respects to the traditional art of ancient Egypt) and the Late Period. There is also the fascinating funerary chamber of Harhotep, from Deir al-Bahari, featuring magnificent decorated furnishings.

The visit continues on the first floor where a separate ticket has to be purchased for the hall containing the mummies. The visitors' attention is generally concentrated on the recently restored halls containing the 2,099 relics of the Treasure of Tutankhamun, discovered by Howard Carter in the Valley of the Kings in 1922. Here the visitor is greeted by a succession of thrilling display cases

*72-73*
*The Geese of Meidum,*
*painted on plaster.*
*4th Dynasty.*

*72 bottom left*
*A detail of the statue of*
*Nofret, from Meidum.*
*4th Dynasty.*

*72 bottom right*
*The Narmer Palette, bas-*
*relief on green schist, from*
*Hierakonpolis.*
*Dynasty 0.*

*73 top*
*Hippopotamus in blue*
*Faience, from the necropolis*
*of Dra Abu al-Naga.*
*Second Intermediate Period.*

with, alongside the relics exhibited and published innumerable times throughout the world, hundreds of other fabulous objects that were intended to accompany the king on his journey to the Afterlife and now compose the richest and most complete funerary cache yet to be discovered in Egypt. As well as the museum's 12 most popular rooms the first floor also offers other funerary treasures of exceptional value, including the particularly interesting collection of Queen Hetepheres of the (mother of Khufu), examples of the goldsmiths' art that cover the history of Egypt from the primordial era through to the Byzantine era and a body of hieroglyphic texts on papyrus taken from

the *Book of the Dead*. This floor is also rich in relics that narrate something of the ordinary lives of the ancient Egyptians, models of armies and homes, tools and jewellery, "minor" objects that are nonetheless capable of captivating the interest of visitors even more than the majesty of the great statues and the dazzling gold.

*73 bottom left*
*Triad of Menkaura, grey-green schist, from Giza.*
*4th Dynasty.*

*73 bottom right*
*Statue of Khafre, in diorite, found at Giza.*
*4th Dynasty.*

**74-75 top**
*Model depicting the
livestock count from
Deir al-Bahari.
11th Dynasty.*

**74-75 bottom**
*Model depicting
a troop of Nubian archers,
from Assiut.
11th Dynasty.*

**75**
*Model of a fishing scene on
the Nile, from
Deir al-Bahari.
12th Dynasty.*

76
Upper part of a sandstone
colossus statue representing
Amenhotep IV,
from Karnak.
18th Dynasty.

77
Unfinished head in
quartzite of Queen
Nefertiti, from
Tell al-Amarna.
18th Dynasty.

**78**
*Solid gold death mask of
Tutankhamun, from the
Valley of the Kings.
18th Dynasty.*

**79 top left**
*Simulacrum of the god
Anubis, in tarred and gilded
wood, from the Valley of the
Kings. 18th Dynasty.*

**79 bottom left**
*Gilded wood statue of the
ka of Tutankhamun, from
the Valley of the Kings.
18th Dynasty.*

**79 right**
*Throne of Tutankhamun,
wood, gold-leaf, semi-precious
stones and vitreous paste, from
the Valley of the Kings.
18th Dynasty.*

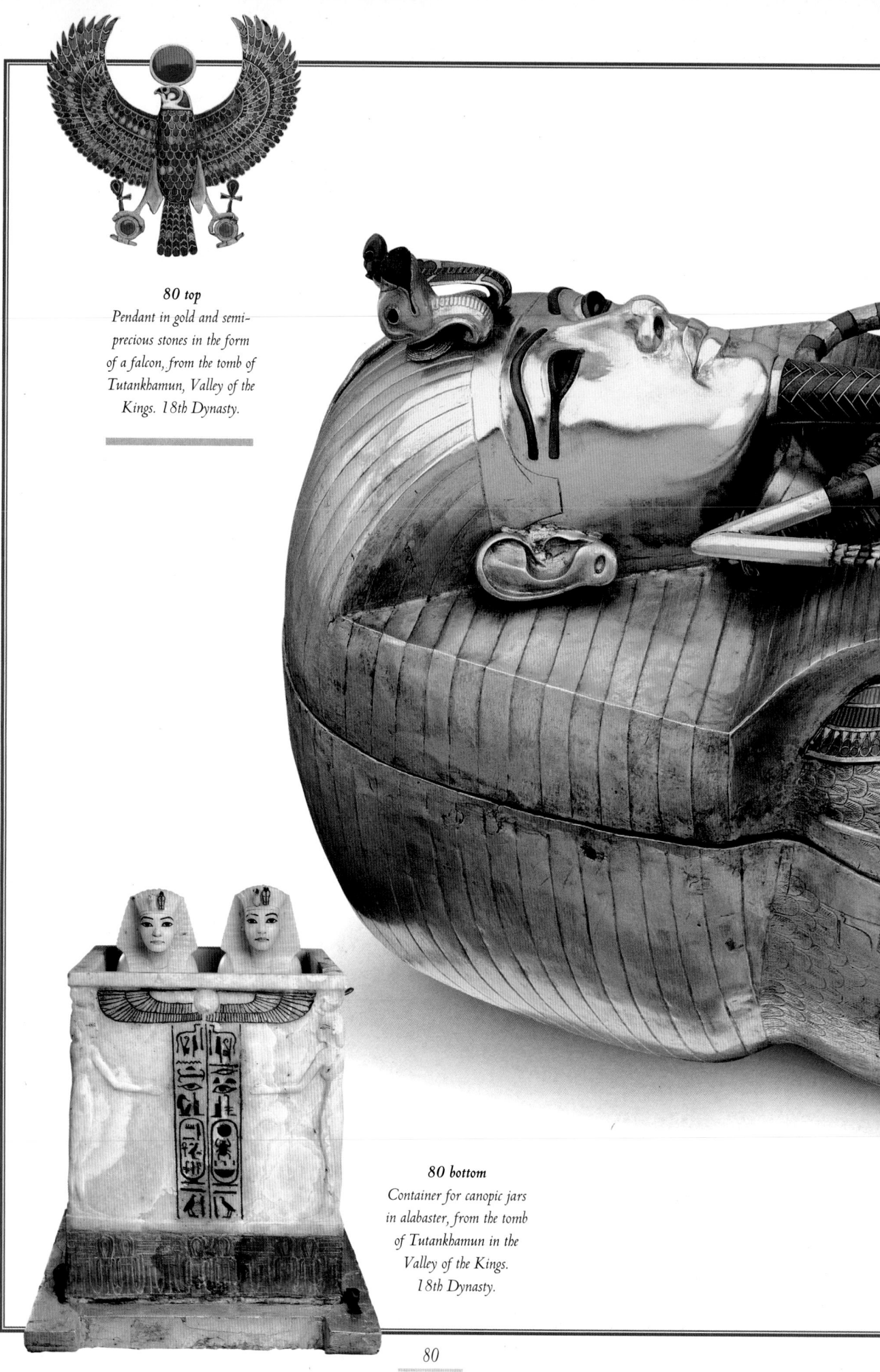

*Shrine in gilded wood for
the canopic jars of
Tutankhamun, from the
Valley of the Kings.
18th Dynasty.*

**80-81**
*Internal coffin in solid gold,
semi-precious stones and
vitreous paste, that
contained the mummy of*
*Tutankhamun. This
extraordinary piece weighs
110.4 kilos. From the
Valley of the Kings.
18th Dynasty.*

**82 left**
*Wooden sarcophagus of Ramsses II, from the Valley of the Kings. 19th Dynasty.*

**82 top right**
*Portrait of a young woman, tempera on wood, from al-Rubayat. Roman Period.*

**82 bottom right**
*Colossal statue in granite and limestone of the young Rameses II and the god Horun, from Tanis. 19th Dynasty.*

**83**
*Portrait of two brothers, encaustic on wood, from Antaeopolis. Roman Period.*

**84-85 and 84 bottom**
*Limestone colossal statue of
Rameses II, 10.3 metres
tall. Now conserved in a
purpose-built modern
construction.*

# *Memphis*

**85 top**
*This great alabaster sphinx is no less than 8 metres long and weighs 8 tonnes.*

**85 bottom**
*Aerial view of the local open-air museum, with the alabaster sphinx.*

The few ruins of Memphis, the capital of the Old Kingdom, are located around 30 kilometres from Cairo, near the village of Al-Badrashein, and not far from the necropolis of Saqqara South. Tradition has it that Memphis was founded by Menes — or Aha, the first king of the 1st Dynasty — for centuries Memphis was the sole capital of Egypt until, at the beginning of the New Kingdom, it was joined by Thebes in the administrative and spiritual leadership of the country. An important religious centre during the Ptolemaic Period, Memphis began to decline in the face of the cultural rise of Alexandria and during the Mameluke dominion it was neglected to the point where it was flooded by the Nile.

Today, visitors can admire, in particular, the prostrate colossal statue of Rameses II sculpted from a single block of calcareous stone and originally 14 m high, and an alabaster Sphinx, with the features of Amenhotep II, opposite the temple of Ptah.

# Saqqara

N ot far from the archaeological area of Memphis, in a westerly direction, lies the necropolis of Saqqara South. The northern part of the area comprises the pryramids of Djedkara Isesi, the 5th Dynasty ruler, and of Pepy I and Merenra, both 6th Dynasty sovereigns. The first is best preserved, but all have lost the interior decoration that featured the sacred Pyramid Texts. These are instead legible in the pyramid of Pepy II, located a short distance to the south. Nearby, the al-Farun mastaba, is the tomb of Shepseskaf, last king of the 4th Dynasty; the two-stepped monument has the rectangular form of a a sarcophagus and is oriented east-west.

Heading north towards Giza you will reach the principal archaeological site of Saqqara housing one of the oldest pharaonic necropolises in Egypt. Like Giza, the complex stands on a plateau raised above the level of the Nile.

Excavations began in 1912, bringing to light in the northern area tombs and mastabas from the 1st Dynasty; the mastaba attributed to Aha was found to contain objects, arms and the oldest papyrus ever to be discovered.

## THE FUNERARY COMPLEX OF DJOSER

The funerary complex of Djoser is the most important monumental work at Saqqara and was built by the vizier Imhotep, an architect and court physician. The oldest of the Egyptian pyramids is enclosed within a rectangular limestone wall, originally decorated with with pilasters and 14 false doors on each face. The very narrow entrance leads into a gallery with 40 clustered pillars arranged in two rows.

The base of the six-stepped pyramid is rectangular and the terraced summit tops out at 58.8 metres. The pyramid was built in five phases, departing from an initial mastaba tomb.

**86 top**
Aerial view of the necropolis
of Saqqara, the largest in
Egypt.

**86 centre**
The remains of the so-called
"royal pavilion" in the
Djoser complex.

**86 bottom**
The entrance opened in the
curtain wall surrounding
the Djoser complex.

**86-87**
The pyramid of Djoser is
the fruit of five successive
enlargements of a mastaba.

**87 bottom**
Another two views of the
funerary complex of
Djoser.

The interior is very complex. The funerary chamber of Djoser is at the bottom of a shaft almost in the centre of the building, while the subterranean sections develop in a labyrinth of corridors, staircases, shafts and chamber over 5 kilometres long.

The stores were contained shards of over 40,000 vases, 4,000 of which have been reconstructed, as well as jugs, plates, trays and sarcophaghi, all funerary furnishings of the wives and children of the king.

In the thre courtyards are the remains of a small temple, the chapels for the celebration of the *Heb-Sed* jubilee festival and two buildings known as the South House and the North House. The Serdab adjoining the north side of the pyramid is interesting: a small sealed chamber containing a statue of Djoser, pierced at the level of the eyes to allow him to maintain a vigil over the world (the sculpture is a copy of the original now conserved in the Museum of Cairo). The remains of the funerary temple are also located on the north side of the pyramid.

The southern side of the Djoser wall contained the enigmatic South Tomb, equipped with a funerary temple (external) and an important hypostyle section at the bottom of a shaft. Beyond the wall, to the south, stands the small, 5th Dynasty pyramid of Unas. While the exterior of this monument is badly damaged, the interior is of great interest. The antechamber and the burial chamber feature well preserved hieroglyphic engravings of passages from the earlier Pyramid Texts. To the south of the enclosure wall of the pyramid of Unis is the tomb of Maya, the treasurer to Tutankhamun: discovered in 1986, the tomb is made of three rooms decorated with hieroglyphs and figured scenes; the sarcophagus and the funerary furnishings can be seen in the Museum of Cairo. Another wide funerary complex is the one attributed to the Sekhemkhet, the successor to Djoser, who ruled for seven years. The enclosure housed a step pyramid; the entrance shaft led to a subterranean area with 132 chambers where an empty alabaster sarcophagus was found.

In the north-east of the site, immediately adjacent to the enclosing wall, are located the ruins of the pyramid of Userkaf (2465-2458 BC), the founder of the 5th Dynasty, and a short distance to the east, the remains of the pyramid of Tety (2323-2291 BC), founder of the 6th Dynasty.

## THE MASTABAS

The mastabas are tombs of a parallelepiped shape, sized according to the importance of their owners. The external structure is composed of one or more chapels giving access to the hypostyle chambers by way of a staircase or a shaft. There are numerous well preserved examples at Saqqara.

The decoration of the mastabas represents the highest expression of the figurative art of the Old Kingdom. Of particular interest is the tomb of Mereruka and his wife Sesheshet. With its 32 rooms, this is the largest and most complex of the Old Kingdom mastabas. Decorations with everyday subject matter such as hunting and fishing scenes, domestic and wild animals, farmers, labourers and craftsmen at work and family portraits have provided Egyptologists with insights into the daily lives of the ancient Egyptians.

Other significant mastabas in the area are those of Kagemni and, in particular, Ty. The fascinating relief decorations in the latter are among the most beautiful from the Old Kingdom.

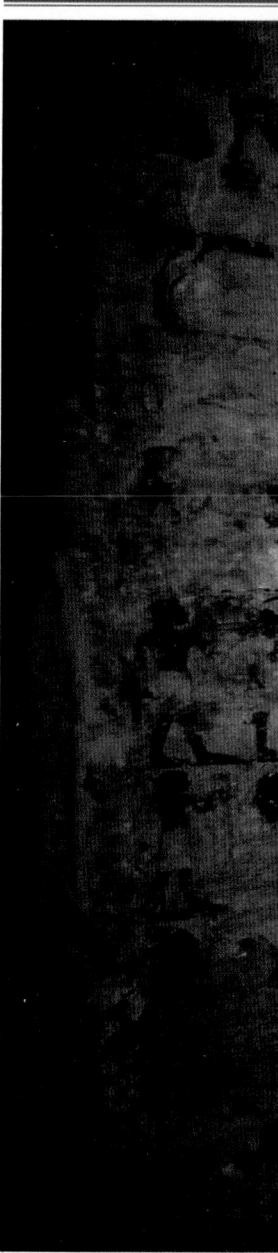

*88 top*
*Bas-relief inside one of the mastabas that surround the funerary complex of Djoser.*

*88 centre*
*Bas-relief inside one of the satellite pyramids of the funerary complex of Djoser.*

**88-89**
*Ten polychrome statues sculpted in the living rock are aligned inside the tomb of Irukaptah.*

**89 bottom left**
*A view of one of the rooms inside the mastaba of Kagemni at Saqqara.*

**89 bottom right**
*Bas-relief depicting a funerary procession, located in one of the private tombs at Saqqara.*

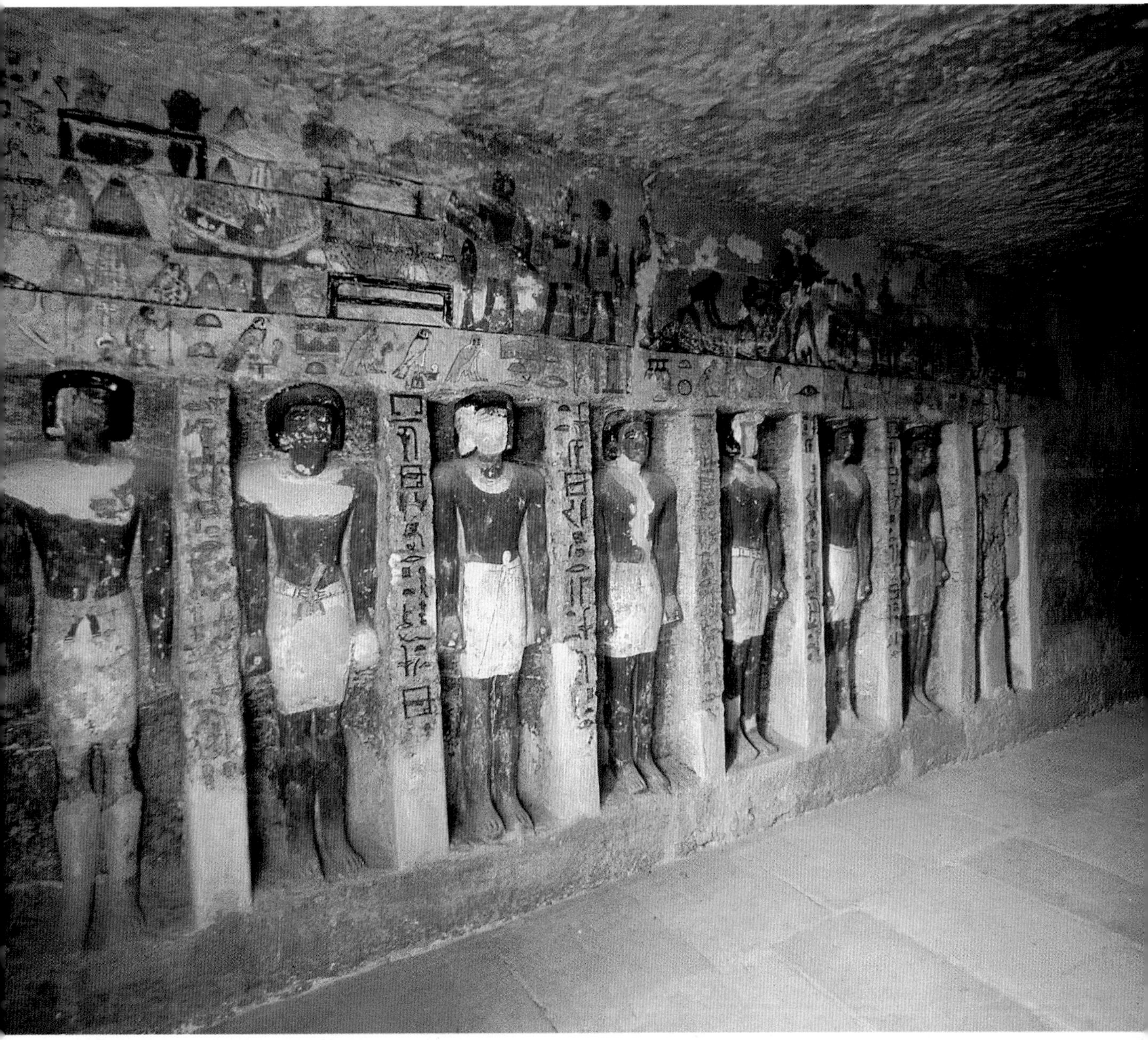

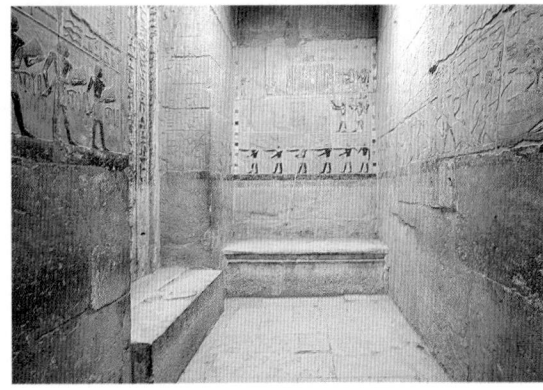

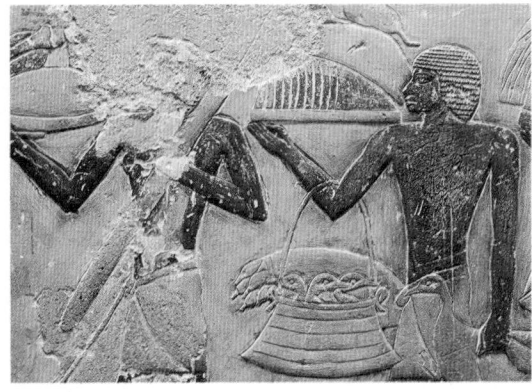

# *Dahshur and surrounding area*

This is the southernmost site of the great Cairo archaeological area and is located a few kilometres south of Saqqara, the royal necropolis of the Old and Middle Kingdoms. Dahshur features five pyramids, all of which are still visible today. Two of these are of great interest and are both attributed to the pharaoh Snefru, the founder of the 4th dynasty (2575-2551 BC). Of the pair, the southern one is known as the "Bent Pyramid" due to the double inclination of its faces, while the second, known as the "Red Pyramid" features the same inclination as the upper section of the Bent Pyramid, but a shallower slope than that of the Great Pyramid at Giza. Both pyramids are over 90 metres high, are built in stone and have an internal burial chamber with a very high ceiling composed of projecting slabs of stone. No sarcophaghi or inscriptions were found inside the Bent Pyramid; however, the excavation brought to light the Lower Temple composed of a courtyard with a colonnade, chambers and chapels with bas-reliefs. The Red Pyramid, so-named after the colour of the stone used, has a broader base and is slightly taller than the bent pyramid. The other three pyramids at Dahshur belong to the pharaohs of the Middle Kingdom, Amenemhat II, Senusret III and Amenemhat III of the 12th Dynasty.

## ABUSIR AND ZAWIYET-AL-ARYAN

While not a habitual stop on the traditional tourist routes, these two sites feature elements of great archaeological interest.

Abu-Sir is the necropolis of the 5th Dynasty;

**90 top**
*Aerial view of the pyramids of Neferirkara (bottom) and Niuserra (top) at Abusir.*

**90 top left**
*The elegant profile of the Red Pyramid at Dahshur.*

**90 centre left**
*Another view of the Abusir complex; on the left note the unfinished pyramid of Neferefra.*

the area of the Solar Temples and lots of pyramids. Most of these are ruined, but the constructions of the pharaohs Sahura, Neferirkara and Nyuserra give precise information about the characteristics of the funerary monuments of the 5th Dynasty (2465-2323 BC). The pharaohs of this dynasty declared themselves to be descendants of the sun god Ra and the temples represented the point of conjunction between the sovereign and his divine origins; the obelisks (known as *tekhen* to the ancient Egyptians) located inside the sanctuary above a truncated pyramid date from this period.

The obelisk was a symbolic representation of the god Ra of Heliopolis and could, like the pyramids, be interpreted as the petrification of the sun's rays or the sacred primordial stone upon

which the sun rose. The monuments found at Abu-Sir are less impressive than those of Giza, but feature a greater stylistic elegance. The austere rectangular pilasters give way to columns representing bundles of reeds with capitals sculpted in the form of date palm leaves. The walls are decorated with bas-reliefs although, unfortunately, most of these were destroyed by the vandalism of the past centuries.

Temples and tombs, at Abu-Sir, are precisely aligned along the course of the Nile, as at Giza. The lower temples were probably lapped by the waters of the river. The excavations prepared for an unbuilt pyramid and the ruins of a second pyramid from the 3rd Dynasty can be found in the Zawiyet-al-Aryan area.

*90 bottom left*
*The unmistakable shape of the Bent Pyramid at Dahshur.*

*90-91*
*Another fine aerial view of the Abusir complex, with the three pyramids surrounded by the vast necropolis.*

# The Oases

The word "oasis" used by the Egyptians and then Herodotus to describe the areas of vegetation in the Libyan Desert to the west of the Nile, meant "cauldron". The oases are, in effect, depressions in the ground that are almost impermeable and therefore rich in wells and springs that since ancient times have permitted the practise of agriculture, and in particularly viticulture. The ancient text of Edfu, dating from the Ptolemaic Period, mentioned seven oases, including those of Kharga, Dakhla, Farafra, Bahariyya, Siwa and Fayum.

These oases were inhabited in prehistoric times and here the organised tribes were more advanced than those of the Nile valley. From the earliest dynasties, the pharaohs made sure they occupied many of these areas given their strategic importance and the value of their inhabitants as desert guides.

## FAYUM

The oasis of Al Fayum is a vast cultivated area to the south-west of Cairo; it is principally irrigated by the Bahr Yussuf (the River of Joseph), a canal linking the oasis to the river and flowing into Birket Qarun (known to the ancients as the Moeris). Traditionally dedicated to the crocodile divinity Sobek, the name of the oasis was derived from the Coptic word *Phiom*, meaning lake or sea, which itself derived from the Egyptian word of the same meaning *Pa iam*. The absence of a flow of water draining the area meant that vast swamps were created arund the oasis with luxuriant vegetation and a richly varied fauna, conditions that made Fayum a favourite hunting area of the pharaohs. A number of 12th Dynasty sovereigns undertook large-scale reclamation projects, increasing the tillable land by means of a complex network of canals and locks that attracted a great number of colonists to the area.

Al Fayum enjoyed a period of great expansion during the Middle Kingdom and, thanks to the ingenious hydraulic systems mentioned by Strabo and Herodotus, Birket Qarun was raised two metres above sea level. The Macedonian, Greek and Hebrew colonists built new cities such as Crocodilopolis, Karanis and Dionysus, while Al Fayum became the centre of Hellenistic culture in Egypt. Numerous Greek and Egyptian papyruses came from these cities, but the most unusual archaeological finds are the numerous portraits of ordinary people executed in encaustic on wood for funerary purposes. The oasis prospered for centuries until the lake shrank to its present size following the administrative decadence that characterised the whole of Egypt in the 3rd century AD.

Karanis features the ruins of the temple of Nero dedicated to the crocodile deities, Pnepheros and Petosuchos. A great number of mummified examples of these reptiles have also been discovered, probably dedicated to Sobek.

**92 top**
*One of the lion-headed sphinxes that adorned the* dromos *of the temple of Medinet Madi in the Fayum.*

**92 centre top**
*The ruins of the north temple of Karanis, in the Fayum.*

Around 10 kilometres to the south-west stand the ruins of Dimet, the ancient Soknopaiu Nesos, or Island of Sobek. On the southern side is the 400-metre long processional avenue running alongside the temple which still contains relief sculptures showing Ptolemy II praying to the god Amun.

Close to the village of Biahmu stood two imposing colossal statues of Amenemhat III which were seen by Herodotus during his journey through Egypt and also mentioned by a traveller in 1700. Today, all that remain here are the bases and a few fragments of the statues currently displayed in the Ashmolean at Oxford. Medinet Al Fayum instead features the obelisk of Senusret I (12th Dynasty), erected at the centre of a cross-roads.

The village of Al Maqta boasts the ruins of the brick pyramid of Hawara, built by Amenemhat III and, further to the south, the few remains of his huge funerary temple with the 12 courtyards which inspired Greek travellers that called it "Labyrinth".

*92 centre bottom*
*The temple of Amenemhat III at Medinet Madi.*

*92 bottom right*
*A view of the Oasis of Fayum.*

*92-93*
*The pyramid of al-Lahun, in the Fayum.*

*93 bottom left*
*The temple of Qasr Qarun in the Fayum.*

*93 bottom centre*
*Interior of the temple of Qasr Qarun.*

*93 bottom right*
*Interior of the temple of Medinet Masi in the Fayum.*

**94**
*The temple of Ibis in the Kharga Oasis.*

**95 top left**
*One of the great gateways in front of the temple of Ibis.*

**95 centre top**
*The ruins of Qasr Dush, a temple dedicated to Serapis, to the south of Kharga.*

**95 centre bottom**
*The Dakhla Oasis: the temple of Deir al-Hagiar.*

**95 top right**
*Polychrome bas-relief inside the temple of Deir al-Hagiar.*

**95 right centre top**
*The Siwa Oasis, with one of the characteristic rocky outcrops.*

**95 right centre bottom**
*The celebrated Temple of the Oracle in the Siwa Oasis.*

**95 bottom right**
*The ruins of the temple of Amun, in the Siwa Oasis.*

## KHARGA

The oases of Kharga and Dakhla, located to the west of Thebes and constantly under Egyptian control, boast ancient monuments still today immersed in unspoilt surroundings. Just to the north of Kharga, known as Al-Khargia in Arabic, rise the ruins of the ancient city of Hibis, with its temple of Amun dedicated to the god by Darius I, restored and extended by Nectanebo II and then further enlarged during the Graeco-Roman Period.

The temple features a classic layout with pylons, courtyard and a hypostyle hall; there is an interesting depiction of the god Seth in the act of transfixing the serpent Apopis with a spear. Seth, a deity initially seen as a benevolent protector of the oases, had a far darker image in the Nile valley. It should be noted that the deity's slaying of the serpent with a spear was a motif taken up in Christian iconography with St. George and the dragon. Around a kilometre to the north of the temple, are the ruins of the Christian necropolis of Al-Baqawat. A number of the chapels have pictorial decorations with biblical themes and symbolic figures, some of which are still well preserved.

## DAKHLA

This oasis, Al-Dakhila in Arabic, is renowned for its great natural beauty and proverbial tranquillity. This is the largest of the oases in the Western Desert and is located around 350 kilometres from the Nile; it was discovered by Bernardino Drovetti of Piedmont in 1819.

There are few ruins in the area: the lythic tomb of Kitines and the remains of the temple of Mut, built during the 18th and 19th Dynasties and subsequently restored by Rameses IX. The mastabas of governors from the Old Kingdom have recently been discovered in situ, confirming the interest the vast oasis held for the ancient Egyptians of the Nile Valley.

## FARAFRA

Farafra or Al-Farafira was known to the ancient Egyptians as "Taith", the "Land of the Cow". Archaeological excavations recently undertaken have identified the remains of houses from Predynastic periods. There is, instead, no trace of the presence of the pharaohs, in spite of the oasis being mentioned in documents from the 5th Dynasty onwards. Close to Qasr Farafra, the interesting town surrounded by walls, stands an ancient necropolis with rock tombs.

## SIWA

It is said that immediately after founding Alexandria, Alexander the Great undertook a long and gruelling journey to the oasis of Siwa in order to consult the oracle of Jupiter-Amemnon.

The oasis of Siwa only came under Egyptian control during the Ptolemaic Period due to its remoteness (551 kilometres from Cairo) and the hostility of the local people. In ancient times, the Libyans and the inhabitants of the oases consecrated it to a native deity called Amemnon by the Egyptians and Greeks. The remains of the temples of Aghurmi and Umm al-Beda, probably dating from the Saitic period, are the only ruins left.

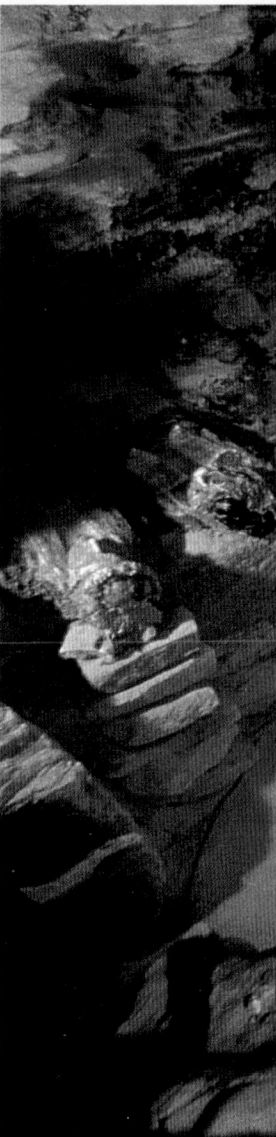

**96 top**
*Bas-relief in a tomb at Beni Hasan.*

**96 centre top**
*The gilded plaster mask of one of the mummies discovered in the Bahariyya Oasis.*

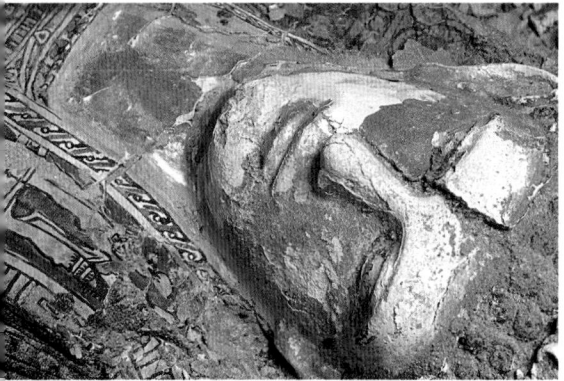

# BAHARIYA (WAHAT AL-) OR BAHRIYYA

Bahriyya means "Oasis of the Sea" or "Northern Oasis" and is situated in a deep depression to the west of Al Fayum. The oasis still houses the remains of a 26th Dynasty temple, inscriptions in the chapel of the pharaoh Apries revealing that the complex was dedicated to Amun-Ra, "Lord of the great hill", and to the god Khonsu who, along with his parents Amun and Mut, was part of the triad of Thebes.

The rock tombs of the nobles situated behind the slope of the village are also interesting, the oldest being that of the governor Amenothep from the 18th Dynasty. Although in poor condition, it still retains some of the original colours.

The burial complex of the ibises at Qarat al-Faragi has to date given up a number of mummified corpses of these birds, as well as amulets. The oasis has aroused international interest both for the remains of its Roman monuments and the very recent discovery of the so-called "necropolis of the golden mummies" by Zahi Hawass's Egyptian team. Over 105 mummies from the Graeco-Roman epoch have been recovered, but it is estimated that there are over 10,000 in total. This necropolis is located close to the temple of Alexander the Great and was discovered by chance in 1996, when a watchman returning home from work with his donkey noticed that the animal's hoof had sunk into the ground. Immediate excavations brought to light a number of mummies.

# BENI HASAN

Beni Hasan is located halfway between the ancient royal cities of Memphis and Thebes, in an area palm groves and green fields close to the Nile. An ancient Middle Kingdom necropolis, its 39 tombs are almost all situated along the side of the hill. Only a few are open to the public, but they are all of interest and contain scenes of agriculture, hunting and sport.

Tomb No. 17, which still has two of its original six columns, features scenes of wrestling,

**96 centre bottom**
*A view of the tomb of Bannantiu, discovered in the Bahariyya Oasis.*

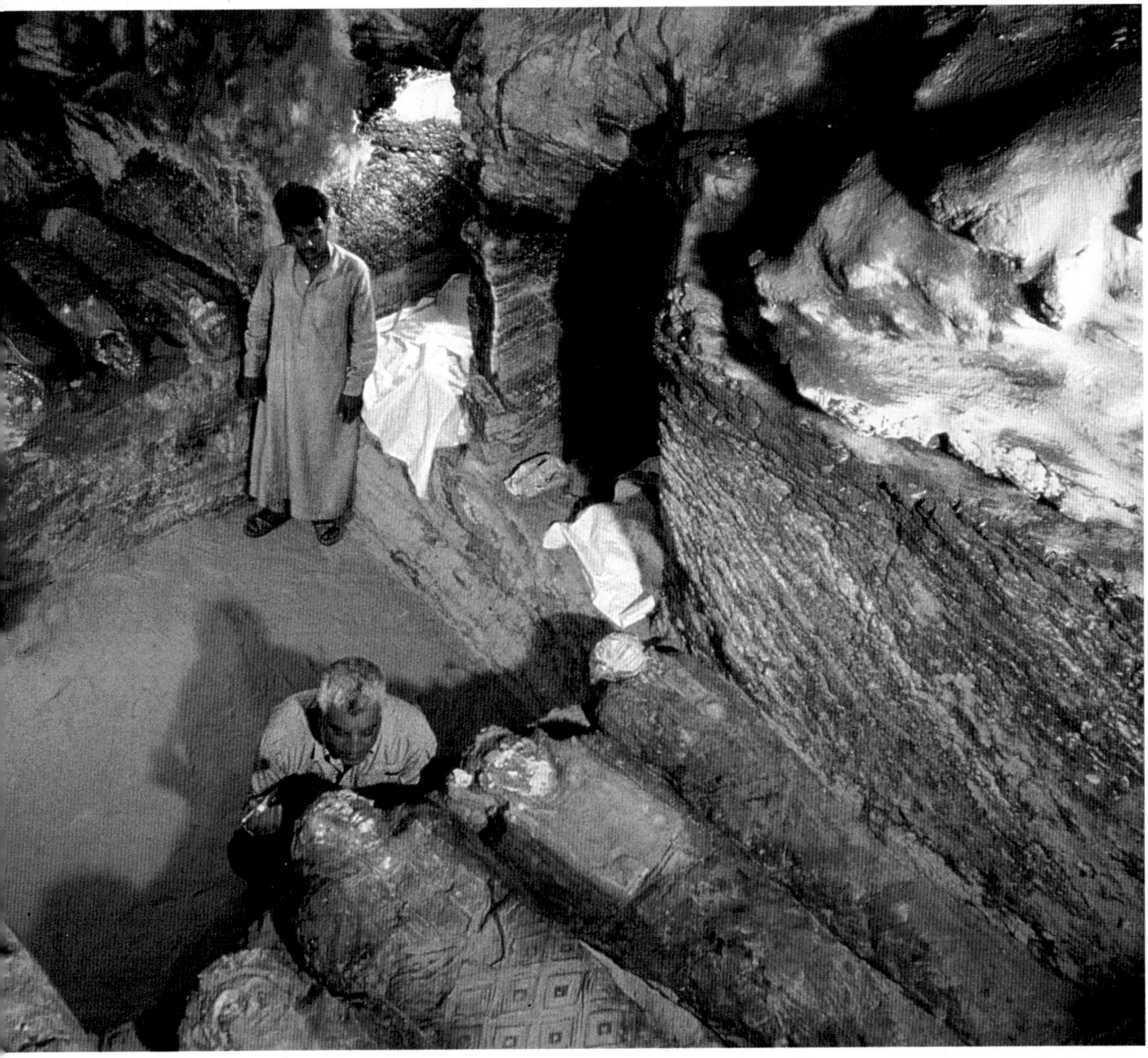

**96 bottom**
*Interior of one of the tombs at Beni Hasan.*

**96-97**
*The Egyptian archaeologist Zahi Hawass cleaning sand from some mummies from the Bahariyya Oasis.*

**97 bottom**
*Another detail of a tomb at Beni Hasan.*

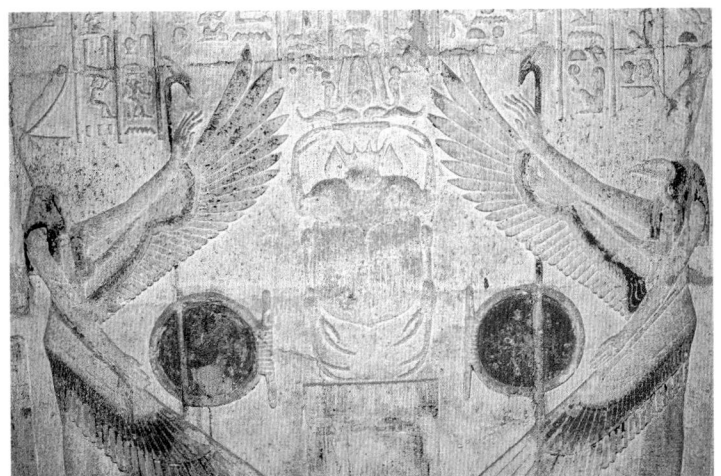

hunting and dance in sequential scenes of movement of such accuracy as to create the impression of cinematic frames. The tomb was constructed at the behest of the high priest Kethi, who is portrayed wearing the typical sacerdotal leopard-skin robes. Tomb No. 15, which belonged to governor of the *nome*, Baket, the father of Kethi, is similar, while Tomb No.3 belonging to Khnumhotep, another local nomarch and governor, is famous for its drawings depicting hunting and fishing scenes. The columns of these hypogea are in the style defined by Champollion as "Proto-Doric". The expedition led by the Frenchman and the Tuscan Ippolito Rossellini between 1828 and 1829, spent much time here and made accurate drawings of the interiors.

In 1891, the Egypt Exploration society despatched the young archaeologist Percy Newbarry to work here with a talented young draughtsman, one Howard Carter.

# Tell al-Amarna

Around 70 kilometres from the city of Al Minya in central Egypt stand the ruins of Akhenaten, capital of the Amarnian religious revolution named after the present day city of Tell al Amarna. The city was founded by the 18h Dynasty pharaoh, Amenhotep IV, better known by the new name he chose for himself, Akhenaten. Close to the present day village of Al Till, the confines of this ephemeral capital are delineated within an area enclosed by rocky walls extending for almost three kilometres along the banks of the Nile. The city was founded on virgin soil and inhabited for no more than thirty years. Amenhotep IV had the courage to make a definitive stand against the power of the Theban sacerdotal class: if is true that this king, apparently a lover of art and nature, rejected the idea of war *a priori*, it is perhaps plausible that the instrument of religion appeared to him to be more efficient and painless. The proclamation of a single god, Aten,

*98 top*
*A surviving column from the great temple of Aten.*

*98-99*
*The stepped path that leads to the rock necropolis.*

*99 top*
*A detail of the polychrome bas-reliefs that decorate the interior of one of the tombs.*

*99 bottom*
*View of the ruins of Tell al-Amarna.*

the solar disc, and the obscuring of all the Theban deities, including Amun, perhaps created a pressing need for a new centre from which to officiate the cult of the sun without having to accept pre-existing architectural compromises. This was probably the reason why the pharaoh abandoned Thebes in around the fifth year of his reign and hurriedly built this new capital as careful study of the ruins has revealed. The city was designed in accordance with the worship of a sun god who, each dawn in a daily cyclical ritual, illuminated the rich colours of the buildings and temples. After its destruction by the Theban avengers, Akhenaten was abandoned and fell into oblivion for centuries.

Towards the end of the 19th century, F. Petrie began a series of systematic excavations with the help of a young artist, Howard Carter, destined to achive immense fame with the discovery of the tomb of Tutankhamun. Subsequently, the site was also studied and excavated by German and British teams. Clear references to the city's foundation were discovered on one of the stelae marking its confines; the hieroglyphs reveal that "on the 13th day of the 8th month of the 6th year [of the king's reign] the king, riding in a golden carriage, left the rich tent where he had spent the night and travelled to mark the confines of the city of Akhenaten. After making offering to the divinity he moved south to a point where the sun's rays indicated to him the southern confines of the city. The sovereign prayed for his royal wife and his children and then swore never to pass these confines."

The temple of Aten was deliberately destroyed following the death of the pharaoh and its stones were reused by Rameses II for his temple at Hermopolis Magna. The foundations reveal the shape of the building, a rectangle 800 by 275 metres. The first pylon was followed by a hypostyle hall, covered on either side with the central nave left open. Then came various courtyards separated by porticoes, with some altars raised on platforms of unfired brick and located along the temple axis in rows of four. The last room was devoted to the liturgical ceremonies concerning the encounter with the deity. Nearby, are the surviving foundations of storerooms that served the religious complex.

The palace featured the royal couple's private courtyards and apartments where archaeologists found the image of Akhenaten and Nefertiti sitting facing each other on a large cushion, surrounded by their six daughters. The image is currently conserved in the Ashmolean at Oxford. The entire residence was decorated with scenes of

nature and everyday life, these last displaying a decisive break with the rigid traditional models. It appears that the sovereigns also chose to have themselves portrayed realistically and we can thus be certain of the remarkable beauty of Nefertiti and the partial physical deformation of her consort. Clay tablets were brought to light in the nearby palace archive that documented, in cuneiform characters, the diplomatic correspondence between the pharaohs Amenhotep III, Akhenaten and Tutankhamun and the Asiatic kings and Syrian vassal states. The most sensational find was made in the proximity of the court buildings: the workshop of the craftsman Thutmosis, containing a number of sculpted busts. One of these, probably belonging to Nephertitis, is coloured and in perfect condition and is on display in the Egyptian Museum in Berlin.

The city's necropolis is to be found in the hills to the east. The tomb paintings, in contrast with those of Thebes, do not contain scenes of the underworld; the so-called process of psychostasia practised before Osiris is completely absent here. The paintings instead show vivid representations of terrestrial life. Many of the tombs were unfinished with few showing signs of actually having been used for a burial. It appears that the Amarnian counter-revolution interrupted the eternal rest the necropolis was designed to guarantee the defunct nobles of the city of the sun.

Akhenaten's mummy has long been sought, both here and at Thebes, but to date the research has proved fruitless, despite the fact that the royal tomb was found in these hills at Darb al Malik.

**100-101**
*The imposing remains of the temple of Rameses II.*

**100 bottom left**
*Bas-reliefs from the temple of Rameses II.*

**100 bottom right**
*Rameses II in front of the offerings to the gods.*

# — Abydos —

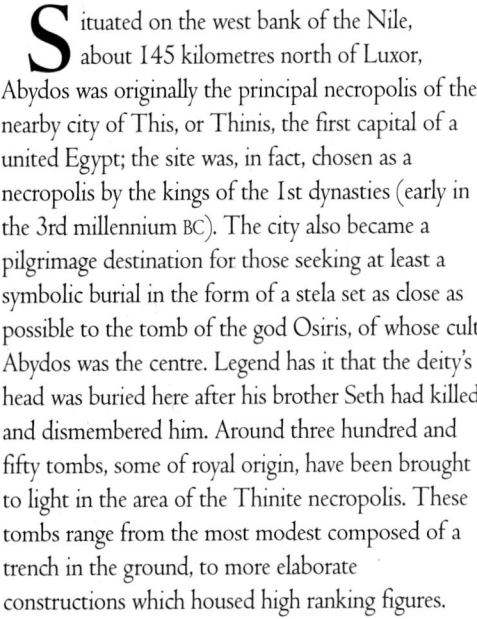

S ituated on the west bank of the Nile, about 145 kilometres north of Luxor, Abydos was originally the principal necropolis of the nearby city of This, or Thinis, the first capital of a united Egypt; the site was, in fact, chosen as a necropolis by the kings of the 1st dynasties (early in the 3rd millennium BC). The city also became a pilgrimage destination for those seeking at least a symbolic burial in the form of a stela set as close as possible to the tomb of the god Osiris, of whose cult Abydos was the centre. Legend has it that the deity's head was buried here after his brother Seth had killed and dismembered him. Around three hundred and fifty tombs, some of royal origin, have been brought to light in the area of the Thinite necropolis. These tombs range from the most modest composed of a trench in the ground, to more elaborate constructions which housed high ranking figures.

Tombs of sacred animals have also been discovered at Abydos, necropolises for jackals, the embodiment of the god Anubis, ibises, the incarnation of the god Thot and the falcons symbolising the god Horus.

## THE TEMPLE OF SETY I

The construction of the Temple of Abydos dedicated to Osiris, was begun by Sety I and completed by his son Rameses II with the addition of a pylon and two courtyards now ruined.

The facade we see today is not the true temple facade, but rather a portico with twelve columns that acted as the backdrop to the second great courtyard. The covered temple and the first hypostyle hall were reached via a ramp. The layout of the building was organised on the basis of the sacred numbers two and seven. There are, in fact, two pylons, two courtyards and two hypostyle halls, seven doors opening onto the internal section and seven bays that traverse the two hypostyle halls and lead to the seven chapels constituting the heart of the temple.

The lateral walls of the first hypostyle hall, with its two transverse rows of twelve columns, and the second with three rows of twelve columns, delineate the passages to the seven shrines dedicated to Sety I, Osiris, Isis, Horus, Amun, Mut and Khonsu. The first hall measuring 52 x 11 metres is divided into seven chapels dedicated to seven different deities; the second hall, the same size as the first, features columns with papyrus capitals and is characterised by a converging floor and ceiling. Of the seven chapels, the one dedicated to Osiris has significant differences compared with the other six which each house a stela on the back wall. In the Osiris chapel instead, a passage opens from the back wall and leads to another temple dedicated to Osiris, Isis and Horus and composed of a principal hall supported by ten columns leading to three chapels. An unusual feature of this secondary temple of Osiris is the presence in the north-west corner of a small room with two columns lacking any form of aperture and therefore inaccessible, as if to symbolise the fact that the secret of the mysteries of Abydos will remain inviolate.

The left-hand part of the temple opens onto a hall with three columns and two chapels consecrated to the gods Nefertim and Ptah Sokaris respectively. Both of these gods were funerary deities associated with the rituals of resurrection.

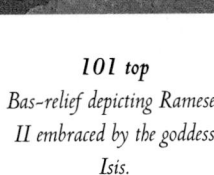

*101 top*
*Bas-relief depicting Rameses II embraced by the goddess Isis.*

*101 bottom*
*The facade of the temple of Sety I, punctuated by 12 pilasters.*

A long corridor leading to the South Halls features a ceiling with stars and royal cartouches, the symbolism of which is explicit: the spirit of the dead king rises to heaven to join the light and become a star. From the corridor once reaches the six southern halls: the first was used a storeroom for the boats used during processions, while the remaining five were used as stores for sacred objects. Leading off this corridor is a flight of steps that once gave access to the roof and which today leads to the cenotaph.

## THE CENOTAPH OF SETY I (OSIREION)

The term cenotaph indicates a particular type of false tomb which does not contain a body, being symbolically dedicated to the deceased's spirit alone. The cenotaph of Sety I at Abydos, to be considered as the spiritual tomb of Osiris dates to before the 19th Dynasty and was discovered in 1903 beneath a vast mass of rubble. Sety I, whose own tomb is located in the Valley of the Kings, transformed this "virtual tomb" into the colossal work we see today. Today the cenotaph is reached by way of the Temple of Sety I, but the original entrance was situated to the north-west of the building and was composed of shafts dug in the desert. This was, in fact, a type of entrance that only the spirit of the deceased was able to penetrate in order to reach the crypt. The nucleus is composed of a hall with ten pilasters symbolising the island at the centre of the world that emerged from the waters at the creation of the universe. During the Nile floods, the cenotaph symbolised an island surrounded by water. The Osireion features two niches, one square and one rectangular, which in all probability contained the sarcophagus and canopic vases of the god Osiris.

Behind the hall with the pilasters is the last hall of the temple, the true inner sanctum, an elongated rectangle in shape with a pitched roof; the hall is decorated with astrological and astronomical inscriptions and images.

## THE TEMPLE OF RAMESES II

The temple of Ramsees II is a small complex around 300 metres north-west of the temple of Sety I, but very little has survived to the present day.

Construction work probably began during the era of Sety I, the resulting monument being one of the principal temples dedicated to Rameses II. The original structure was composed of two pylons and two courtyards, an entrance hall with a single portico, two hypostyle halls and a shrine with three chapels. The first pylon and the first courtyard have been lost and visitors therefore enter the complex through the second pylon which is itself ruined. The second courtyard was distinguished by the presence of twenty-six Osirian columns. Numerous relief sculptures show scenes of ritual sacrifices and offerings to the gods. The upper part of the temple has collapsed, thus depriving us of the scenes which once decorated the hypostyle halls and the shrine.

# Dendera

The city of Dendera is located around 60 kilometres north of Luxor: on the site of the ancient Junet, capital of the sixth nome of Upper Egypt all that remains today is a Ptolemaic Period temple dedicated to the goddess Hathor and dating from the 1st century BC.

The goddess Hathor, symbolically represented by a woman with the ears of a cow, was venerated here as the divinity of the cosmos in which life takes form. Hathor (whose name means Temple of Horus) in fact represents the maternal womb in which Horus — life itself —

was conceived. Hathor is also known as the goddess of love, the source of joy for living creatures. It is no coincidence that one of her most frequent symbols is a *sistrum*, a musical instrument whose vibrations dispersed negative influences and attracted positive ones. The Temple of Dendera is known as the Sistrum Temple as it was conceived as an enormous musical instrument in which the harmonies of the cosmos were brought together.

The building was originally surrounded by triple curtain walls built of brick, but only the Hathor wall around the heart of the sacred complex survives today. Within the walls stood a sacred lake — upon which scenes from the mysteries of Osiris were represented, with the lake becoming the primordial ocean, source of life — and two *mammisi* (temples of birth).

The facade of the temple features six columns representing the goddess' musical instruments, surmounted by the head of Hathor; for each sistrum there are four heads facing towards the four cardinal points.

The entrance to the covered temple gives onto a hypostyle hall, where two groups of nine columns stand either side of the central axis. The ceiling is painted with cosmic and astrological scenes, while heaven is represented by the goddess Nut, who each evening swallowed the sun in order to regenerate it during the night and restore it to the world the following morning.

There follows the hall of apparitions with the ceiling supported by six columns and with three rooms on either side: on the left is the workshop, on the right the treasury where the alchemists produced unguents, oils and precious materials. There follow the calendar and Nile rooms, which had the function of measuring the

**104-105**
*The 42-metre wide temple
facade.*

**105 bottom left**
*The intercolumns of the
mammisi, covered with reliefs.*

**105 bottom right**
*The rear facade of the temple
of Hathor.*

**106**
*The ceiling of the great hypostyle hall, with the astronomical decorations.*

**107 *right centre top***
*A polychrome relief showing the solar disc of Amun-Ra that illuminates the goddess Hathor.*

**107 *left***
*Magnificent examples of Hathoric capitals.*

**107 *right centre bottom***
*The entrance of the Hathoric chapel.*

**107 *top right***
*A series of bas-reliefs inside the* mammisi.

**107 *bottom right***
*The corridor running around the perimeter of the* naos.

rhythm of the seasons to which the prosperity of the country was closely bound. The central room or Ennead Hall, was the place in which a hymn was recited to reawaken the divinity.

Below the temple are twelve crypts set on three levels and representing the underworld. The small rooms were used to conserve the objects required for the cult of the goddess and were considered to be the places in which the divine forces regenerated themselves in silence.

The top of the temple is in part occupied by the terrace destined for the annual celebration of the union with the solar disc, when the statue of the goddess was directly exposed to the sunlight so that it could be "charged" with positive energy. To the north of the terrace, a chapel dedicated to Osiris — a place symbolically associated with resurrection — is particularly interesting because it features a copy of the celebrated circular zodiac, the only such example realised in Egypt. The original is now conserved in Paris. In 1820, Sebastien Saulnier, a member of the French parliament, instructed the builder Jean Baptiste Lelorrain to remove the zodiac. Lelorrain eventually succeeded after a four-week struggle. The zodiac reached Paris in the January of 1822 and

was acquired by the king for the royal library. It was finally transferred to the Louvre in 1919. The sandstone bas-relief measures 2.55 x 2.53 metres, with the central disc having a diameter of 1.55 metres. The circle containing the astronomical representation supported by four pairs of falcon-headed deities and the four divinities of the cardinal points.

A sacred building dedicated to the birth of Isis, the great sovereign spirit of the sacred sites of Egypt and the bringer of life, was erected behind the great temple of Hathor.

Two unusual buildings are to be found at Dendera: the first, to the right of the great courtyard, is the sanatorium where the sick came for thermal treatment (it was not a public building as it was located within the temple walls), while the second is the *mammisi* (the "House of Birth"), a place consecrated to the celebration of the birth of a son conceived by the gods.

The significance of the *mammisi* (a building typical of the Egyptian temples of the Graeco-Roman Period) is illustrated by the relief sculptures that decorate it: a sacred marriage and the birth of a divine son, with specific references to the youth of the creator gods.

# *Luxor*

**108 top**
One of the human-headed
sphinxes that stand before
the temple of Montu.

**108 bottom**
The first pylon of the
Temple of Karnak, preceded
by the avenue of sphinxes.

A rriving at Luxor in the evening, with the sun setting behind the mountains that conceal the desert, one cannot help being entranced by the gently blending of the colours that rapidly transform the landscape.

The Nile flows slowly and lights in the first houses among the palms on the west bank begin to be lit. If we then look up at the almost always clear sky, we see a particularly bright star descend slowly in the midnight blue before disappearing, much later, behind the western mountains. This star was known to the ancient Egyptians as Sothis and was associated with Isis.

This spectacle has been repeated for millennia, long before Theses, Luxor and Karnak came into existence. Thebes, the magnificent and wealthy capital of the glorious dynasties and princes who liberated Egypt from the invaders, white Thebes of the hundred doors celebrated by the Greeks, the sacred city of Amun, Mut and Khonsu, is no more.

Today, all that remains of ancient Thebes are the temples of Karnak and Luxor, together with a few other ruins which we can still admire but which we are obliged to recognise as mere fragments of past splendours.

**108-109**
The eighth pylon of the
Temple of Karnak; on the
left looms the great first
pylon.

**109 bottom left**
The immense statue of
Rameses II located in the
great courtyard.

**109 bottom right**
One of the sphinxes aligned
in the great courtyard.

# THE TEMPLE OF KARNAK

The stones of the vast archaeological area of Karnak recount well over thirteen centuries of history. The buildings here range from the early foundations of the temple erected in the Middle Kingdom to the first pylon probably constructed during the late 30th Dynasty. The god of war, Mont, associated with Thebes during the Old Kingdom, was the first to suffer from the overwhelming rise of the cult of Amun during the Middle Kingdom, as testified by the construction of temples facing west. With the expulsion of the Hyksos from the country and beginning of the 18th Dynasty, "Ipet Isut" or the "Elected Place", became the most important sanctuary in Egypt from spiritual, political and economic points of view.

Amun was considered to be the god that conquered the enemies of Egypt and the various pharaohs such as Amenhotep and Thutmosis I built chapels around pre-existing monuments, identifying themselves in the form of this divinity.

Queen Hatshepsut added two obelisks in front of the ones installed by her father; Thutmosis III enriched Karnak with the building of the southern *propylaeum* that led, via the avenue of Sphinxes, to the temple of the mother goddess, Mut. During the centuries between the pharaoh's Asian conquests and the reign of Amenhotep III, art and architecture saw the establishment of the so-called imperial style, seen at Karnak in the third pylon built by Amenhotep III.

Work began on the great hypostyle hall, subsequently extended by Sety I and his son Rameses II. Foreign influences favoured by the

**110 top**
*The capitals of the central nave have a diameter of 15 metres at the summit.*

**110 bottom**
*The statue of Rameses II and, in the background, the columns of the hypostyle hall.*

### LEGEND
A   Access dromos
B   Enclosure wall of Precinct of Amun
C   Temple of Rameses III
D   Great hypostyle hall
E   Obelisks
F   Wadjit (small hypostyle hall)
G   Courtyard of the Middle Kingdom
H   Akhmenu
I   Temple of Ptah
J   Sacred Lake
K   Temple of Opet
L   Temple of Khonsu
M   Seventh pylon
N   Eighth pylon
O   Ninth pylon
P   Tenth pylon
Q   First pylon (of Nectanebo I)
R   Second pylon
S   Third pylon
T   Fourth pylon

empire brought new wealth to the country and
Amun, who had accompanied and lent strength to
the pharaoh's military campaigns, saw the temple
of Karnak, with its sacerdotal castes and the old
aristocracy that had supported it, extend its power
until it became a centre of power in the country. At
the height of its glory, the temple possessed around
81,000 slaves with their families, 240,000 head of
livestock and 83 ships, and also received tributes of
gold, silver, jewels and precious stones from over
65 cities around the country.

In this period there was an increasingly clear
distinction between the interests of the pharaoh
and those of the sacerdotal class; the inevitable
conflict was to explode over the following years
under Amenhotep IV, son of Amenhotep III.
During his reign a radical religious upheaval took
place that was to torment Egypt for almost a
quarter of a century. Initially, the new pharaoh also

*110-111*
*A 21-metre high column
stands in the great
courtyard, the sole
surviving element of a
kiosk built at the behest of
the Ethiopian king
Taharqa around 680 BC.*

*111 bottom*
*A suggestive view of the
great hypostyle hall.*

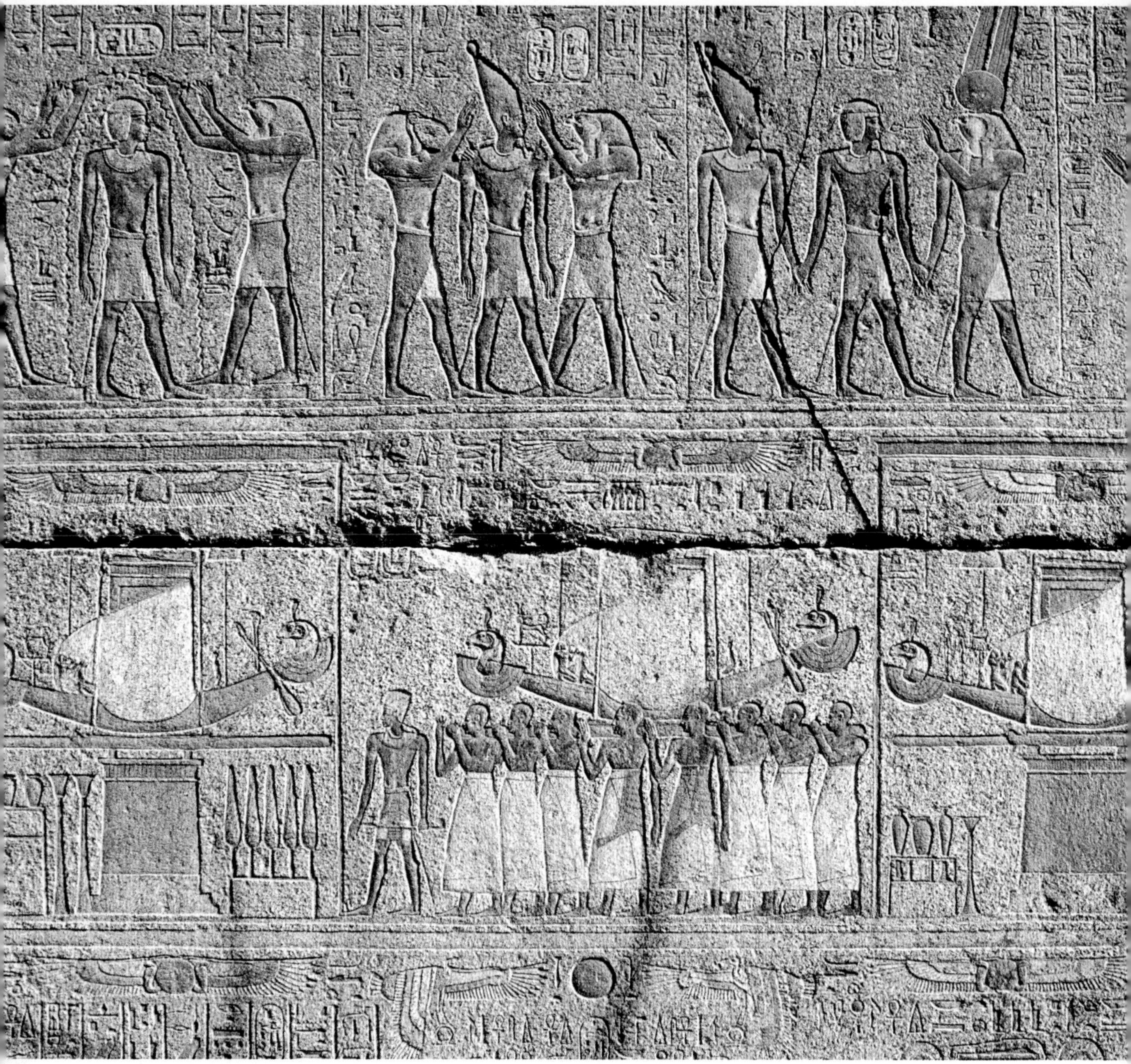

**112-113**
*Bas-relief inside the naos in which is depicted the coronation of Philip Arrhidaeus (upper register) and a procession of priests transporting the sacred barque (lower register).*

**112 bottom**
*One of the thousands of bas-reliefs decorating the Temple of Karnak.*

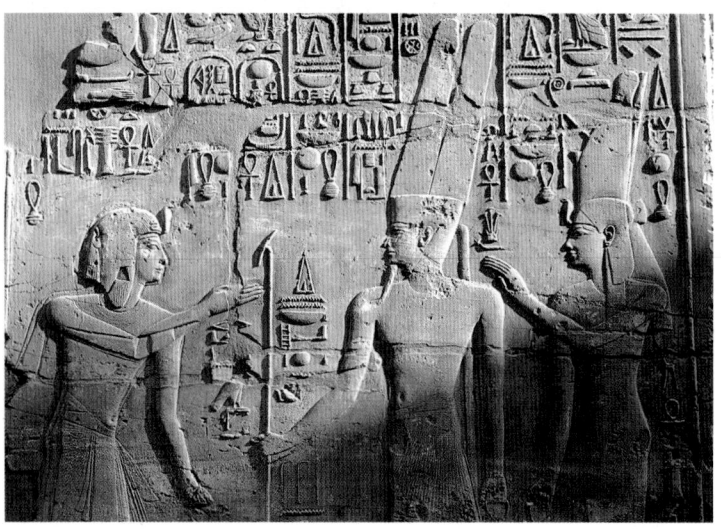

undertook building work at Karnak, but soon transferred the centre of power to a site in central Egypt where he intended to build the new city of Akhenaten. The sovereign's new name, Akhenaten, the pharaoh who revealed to the country the cult of Atun, was incised for the first time on the stelae on the east side of the new city. The pharaoh changed his "Horus name" (Powerful Bull With Tall Feathers) which was too closely associated with Thebes, to "Powerful Bull Beloved of Atun", and his "Nebty name" (Great Regal One of Karnak) into "Great Regal One of Akhenaten.

The temple at Karnak suffered severely as a result of this decision, as in transferring the seat of power the pharaoh erased centuries of history and religious tradition, expunging at a stroke the strong religious power of the Amun priesthood. The new religion failed to survive Akhenaten's death, however; the reign of Tutankhamun saw the restoration of the ancient traditions, with Thebes once again becoming the capital of the kingdom and the temple of Karnak reacquiring all its old power. The works of Akhenaten were completely demolished, the stones of his temples being used to reconstruct later shrines.

The second pharaoh of the 19th Dynasty defined his era as "the repeated rebirths", that is to say, the era of the renaissance. Both he and his son, Rameses II, enriched Karnak with exceptional buildings. The most grandiose and widely admired work was the completion of the enormous central hypostyle hall.

It was the task of the four successive dynasties to construct the first pylon and the large courtyard and thus bring Karnak to its present size. Even though this marked the onset of a long decline, the cult of Amun continued to enjoy undisputed power, with the pharaoh becoming a mere instrument in the hands of this powerful oligarchy.

*113 top*
*The two obelisks erected by Thutmosis I and Queen Hatshepsut.*

*113 centre*
*The cuspidate tip of the obelisk of Thutmosis I.*

*113 bottom*
*Relief depicting the god Thot, inside the chapel of Hatshepsut.*

**114 top left**
*One of the great flights of steps that led to the roof of the grandiose temple.*

**114-115**
*A panoramic view of the Temple of Karnak, with the sacred lake in the foreground.*

**114 bottom left**
*The Osiris pillars in the courtyard of the temple of Rameses III.*

**114 bottom right**
*One of the two pillars with the heraldic symbols of Upper and Lower Egypt erected by Thutmosis III.*

**115 top**
*The Akh-Menu or feasting hall of Thutmosis III, supported by 20 columns and 32 pilasters.*

**115 bottom**
*The god Amun-Ra was the principal divinity worshipped at Karnak.*

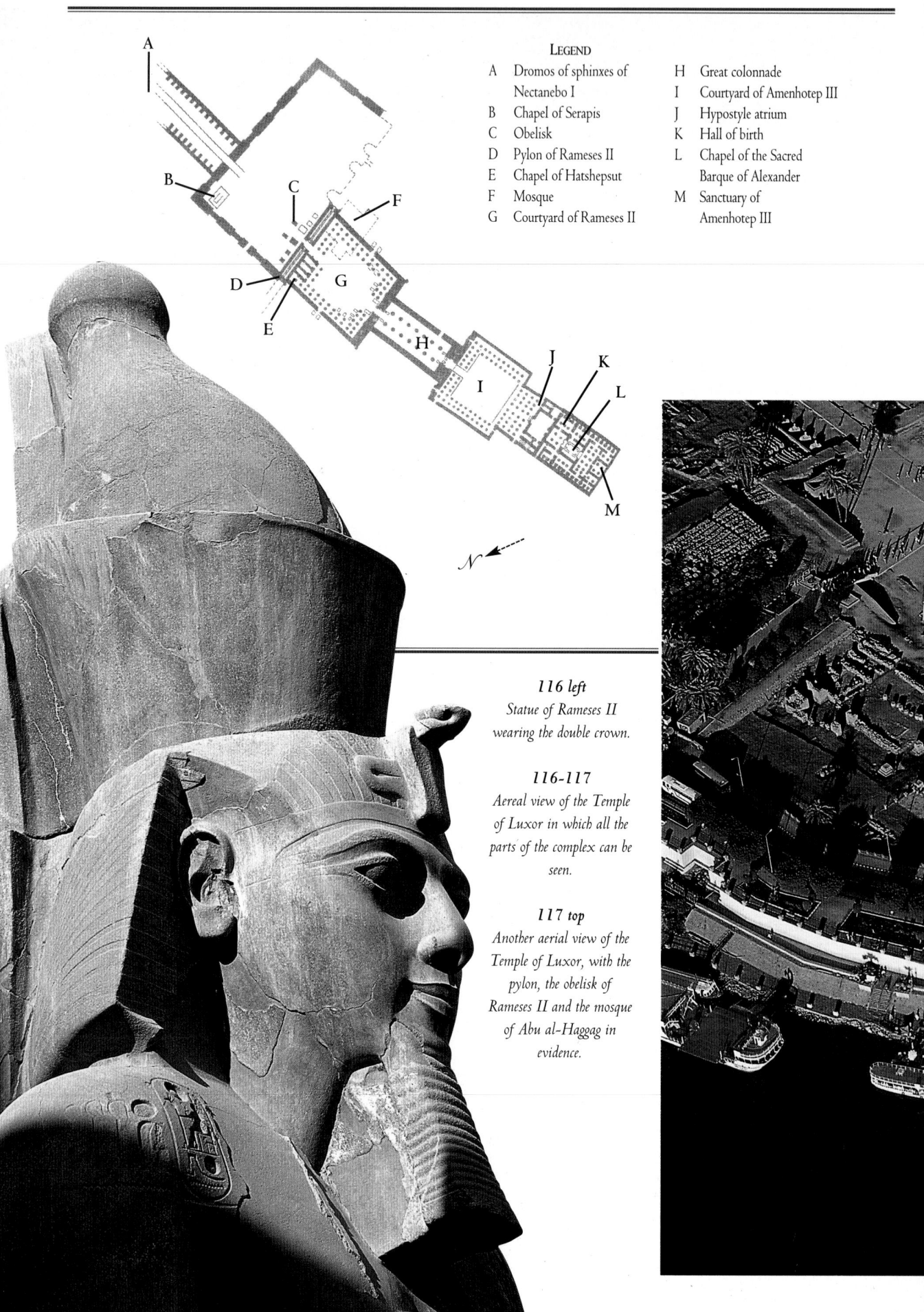

LEGEND

A  Dromos of sphinxes of Nectanebo I
B  Chapel of Serapis
C  Obelisk
D  Pylon of Rameses II
E  Chapel of Hatshepsut
F  Mosque
G  Courtyard of Rameses II

H  Great colonnade
I  Courtyard of Amenhotep III
J  Hypostyle atrium
K  Hall of birth
L  Chapel of the Sacred Barque of Alexander
M  Sanctuary of Amenhotep III

*116 left*
Statue of Rameses II
wearing the double crown.

*116-117*
Aereal view of the Temple
of Luxor in which all the
parts of the complex can be
seen.

*117 top*
Another aerial view of the
Temple of Luxor, with the
pylon, the obelisk of
Rameses II and the mosque
of Abu al-Haggag in
evidence.

## THE TEMPLE OF LUXOR

Luxor's the present-day name derives from *Al Uqsor*, the Arab plural of *qasr* meaning castle, construction, and dates from the era of the emperor Diocletian.

The temple of Luxor was constructed almost entirely during the 18th Dynasty by Amenhotep III and Ramsees II and stands on the foundation of an earlier shrine. Under Amenhotep III it became the centre of political and religious power for the whole country. It was here that the major religious celebrations were held: during the Nile flood seasons the gold statue of Amun was carried on its sacred barque from Luxor to Karnak. In the mystic atmosphere of the temple, the pharaoh

offered gifts and incense to the statue of the god draped in linen. The sacrifices and ceremonies having been completed, the priests carried the deity outside, purifying the road, and then replaced the statue in its barque and returned in procession to Karnak.

Amenhotep was the first pharaoh of the new kingdom to construct monuments of exceptional size designed to convey the new imperialistic ambitions.

Thutmosis III, Hatshepsut and Tutankhamen contributed to the enlargement of the temple, but it was the great Rameses II who was responsible for substantial additions in the form of two majestic pylons, which he himself defined as "the horizon

from which enters the Sun God", and the vast entrance courtyard. These works of clear military propaganda recount, like the famous "poem of Pentaur", the pharaoh's victory against the Hittites in the battle of Qadesh. Modern Egyptologists nonetheless harbour serious doubts regarding the result of the battle. Of the two 25-metre Ramesside pylons, which up until the first half of the 19th century adorned the entrance to the temple, only one remains in its original position; the second was donated to France by Mohammed Ali in 1831 and erected in Place de la Concorde in Paris.

Beyond the pylons and the courtyard stands

**119 bottom centre**
*Another view of the human-headed sphinxes which line the access avenue to the temple.*

**119 bottom**
*A view of the great colonnade no less than 19 metres high erected at the behest of Amenhotep III.*

**118-119**
*The avenue of sphinxes that links the Temple of Luxor (in the background) with that of Karnak.*

**119 top**
*One of the numerous sphinxes located in front of the great pylon of the Temple of Luxor.*

**119 top centre**
*An axial view of the temple from the south-west.*

the colonnade of Amenhotep III, featuring papyrus columns around 16 metres high. The true temple begins to unfold with the first antechamber, once protected by a roof supported on eight columns and which later became a chapel for the cult of imperial Rome. Amenhotep III offering gifts and incense to Amun can still be seen in the second antechamber, immediately after which one enters the shrine-chamber of the holy barque of Amun, reconstructed by Alexander the Great and covered with relief sculptures showing the Macedonian emperor making offerings to various deities including the ithyphallic Min.

**120 top left**
The colonnade of Amenhotep
III, seen from the great
courtyard of Rameses II.

**120 centre left**
A view of the courtyard of
Rameses II, with the nort
side of the pylon; on the left
is the sustaining wall of the
mosque of Abu al-Haggagh.

**120 bottom left**
Detail of the columns
enclosing the courtyard of
Amenhotep III.

**120 right**
The great pylon of the temple,
fronted by the colossal
statues and obelisk of
Rameses II.

**121**
The base of the obelisk and
one of the two colossal
statues of Rameses II that
stand in front of the pylon.

**122 left**
*Statue of Amenhotep III.
18th Dynasty.*

**122 right**
*Black granite statue of the
goddess Iwnit. Reign of
Amenhotep III.*

**123 top left**
*A view of the New
Museum inaugurated in
1975.*

**123 bottom left**
*A general view of the new
gallery.*

**123 centre**
*Sculptural group depicting
Amenhotep III and the
crocodile-headed god Sobek.*

**123 right**
*Statue of a high ranking
dignitary. Reign of
Thutmosis IV.*

## THE MUSEUM OF LUXOR

Inaugurated in 1975, the Museum of Luxor conserves a wealth of exceptional relics ranging from jewellery, furniture and pottery through to stelae and, in particular, boasts statues and busts of great sovereigns such as Senusret III and Thutmosis III (this last, in black basalt, is one of the most beautiful and best preserved ever found), Amenhotep II and Amenhotep III. Also worthy of note is an alabaster statue of Sobek, sculpted during the reign of Amenhotep III and was successively usurped by Rameses II. Characterised by a human body and a crocodile's head, it is an example of the mastery of Egyptian art during the period of its highest expression.

Mural reliefs representing Akhenaten and Nefertiti in adoration of the solar disc Atun are of notable importance. The sculptures were discovered at Karnak in blocks and skilfully reconstructed here. Visitors may also admire the remarkable statuettes of Tutankhamen in his youth and one of the pharaoh's quivers with a set of arrows discovered in his tomb. An engraving on pink granite tells the story of Queen Hatshepsut's expedition to the land of Punt and the subsequent erection of two obelisks giving thanks to Amun in the temple of Karnak.

In the courtyard in front of the museum are two statues of Amenhotep III and Rameses II.

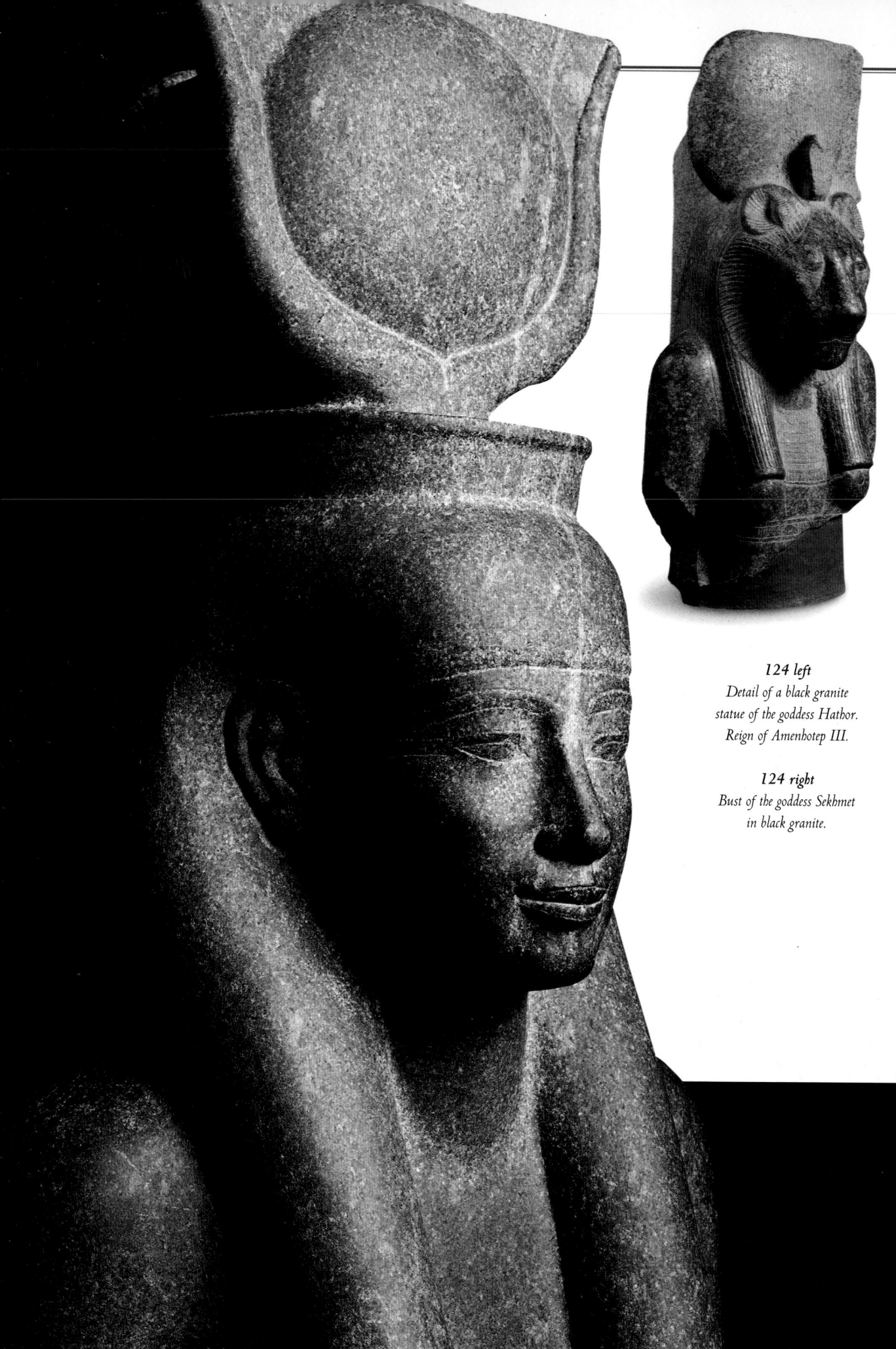

**124 left**
*Detail of a black granite
statue of the goddess Hathor.
Reign of Amenhotep III.*

**124 right**
*Bust of the goddess Sekhmet
in black granite.*

**125 top left**
*Small model boat, from the*
*tomb of Tutankhamun in*
*the Valley of the Kings.*

**125 bottom left**
*Alabaster sphinx, from the*
*tomb of Tutankhamun.*

**125 right**
*Wooden shwabty figure*
*found in the tomb of*
*Tutankhamun.*

# *Western*
# *— Thebes —*

The kings of the 18th, 19th and 20th Dynasties built their tombs on the opposite side of Thebes, on the west bank of the Nile, in the silence of valleys hidden amidst the red and sun-baked mountains. Foregoing any form of external monumentality, they privileged polychrome internal decoration.

The choice of the lone valleys and the concealment of the entrances to the tombs with stones and detritus was evidently intended to avoid the already frequent violations. In the Valley of the Kings, religious tradition was satisfied by the western location of the tombs and underlined by the presence within the mountain range of an almost pyramidal peak, now known as al-Qurn. Visible from almost every point of the valleys, the peak was the petrification of the solar rays according to the symbolism of the Old and Middle Kingdoms.

Western Valley

KV no. 62
Tutankhamun

Valley of the
Kings

Deir
el-Medina

Valley of the
Queens

Medinet Habu
*Temple of
Ramesses III*

Malqatta Royal
Palace of
Amenophis III

**126 top**
*The burial chamber in the
tomb of Tausert.*

**126 bottom**
*Panoramic view of the
Valley of the Kings.*

126-127

*Map of Western Thebes, with the
positions of the funerary temples
and principal necropolises.*

Deir
el-Bahri

Temple of
Hatshepsut

Tombs Of Eleventh's
Dynasty Nobles

Mr Howard Carter's
Residence

Temple of
Mentuhotep

El-Asasif

Dra Abu el-Naga

Metropolitan
Museum House

El-Khokhah

Sheikh Abd
el-Qurna

Upper
Enclosure

Lower
Enclosure

Temple of
Sethos I

Qurna
Village

Temple of
Tuthmosis III

lemaic
ple

Temple of
Amenophis II

Ramesseum

Temple of
Tuthmosis IV

Temple of
Merneptah

Temple of
Amenophis III

E.A.O. Office
(Egyptian
Antiquities
Organizations)

Colossi of
Memnon

mple of the
thmosids

# The Temples
## of
## Western Thebes

The pharaohs of the New Kingdom built their magnificent temples on the west bank of the Nile, at the edge of the cultivated land and in front of the Theban mountain. They all shared an east-west orientation.

The Theban temples had a different function to those of Giza and Saqqara that were constructed for funerary rituals and the cult of the pharaoh after his death. At Thebes instead, these buildings were intended to be used for the cult of the divine king while he was still alive and as memorials for the successive generations.

The magical rituals of the *Heb Sed* jubilee celebrations were conducted here on the occasion of the pharaoh's 30th year on the throne. An, ancient tradition, they were intended to regenerate the spirit of the pharaoh and restore the vital energies crucial to the government and survival of the country.

## THE COLOSSI OF MEMNON

Memnon, the son of Aurora, is a figure in Greek mythology cited by Homer as the King of the Ethiopians, but had nothing to do with the two colossus statues named after him but portraying the pharaoh Amenhotep III. They dominate the entrance to a great temple of which nothing is left.

The colossi stand isolated on the plain one crosses to reach Medinet Habu and, standing around 18 metres high, they are imposing. They first became famous in the Roman era when, due

to an earthquake, they cracked and as a result of thermal dilation and the morning breezes the norther, colossus began to emit sounds similar to a lament, a phenomenon which the Greeks tried to explain as the god Memnon greeting his mother at dawn. The two statues were also situated on a very busy road that led to the south and had become a stopping-off place for the curious who rarely failed to leave evidence of their passing in the form of celebrated graffiti (over 100 examples have been found, including that of the emperor Hadrian).

## THE RAMESSEUM

The temple of Rameses II is part of a complex built by the pharaoh at Thebes West which included stores, enclosures for the temple materials and homes for the servants of the temple. The imposing remains have been an attraction for travellers throughout the ages; the graffiti on the walls testify to the great number of visitors including Diodorus Siculus and G.B. Belzoni.

Commissioned by the British, in 1818 Belzoni succeeded in the arduous task of removing and embarking an enormous bust of the pharaoh which had lain since time immemorial in the courtyard in front of the temple and to send it to the British consul in Cairo, H. Salt. The bust was then moved to England and is today in the British Museum.

The plan of the site follows the classical layout: two successive courtyards, each preceded by a pylon, lead to a large hypostyle hall which in turn leads to a second, smaller hall in front of the shrine dedicated to Amun. The side walls of the temple feature Ramesside propaganda regarding the battle of Qadesh fought against the Hittites in present-day Syria. The relief sculptures show the four Egyptian armies involved in the battle and the king, depicted with giant-like proportions, who from his chariot wipes out entire platoons of minuscule enemies. There is an interesting sense of movement given to the scene through the representation of the horse's hooves, although in reality the Egyptian artists adopted this technique for different motives. They would repeatedly depict an object in order to indicate a plurality, an interpretation confirmed by careful examination of the animal's head where the faint outline of a second head can also be seen. Another significant detail, and one unique to the temples of Ramses, is the figure of Amun in the act of writing the pharaoh's name on a small tablet.

In front of the second pylon can be seen the remains of a huge statue of Rameses II; it probably cracked as a result of an earthquake—18th century drawings show it already in its present position. A project is currently under development to raise the statue to its original erect position, recomposing the various parts still scattered around the site.

## THE TEMPLE OF SETY I

While requiring a slight diversion from the road leading to the Valley of the Kings, the temple of Sety I is well worth visiting. Many of the most beautiful buildings of the New Kingdom such as the temple at Abydos and the hypostyle hall at Karnak have been attributed to this pharaoh. Of the funerary temple at Western Thebes remains the covered temple, while the pylons and courtyards that once stood in front of it have been lost. Relief sculptures representing Sety I and Rameses II as children nursed respectively by Hathor and Mut reveal a regenerative significance in the building. The temple was principally consecrated to Amun, Ra-Horakty and the deified Rameses I, founder of the 19th Dynasty, and the father of Sety I. However, the ruins also comprise areas dedicated to Atum and the warrior god Montu.

# THE SITE OF MEDINET HABU

During the Ramesside Period, Medinet Habu was an important economic and religious centre and home to the pharaoh, the vizier and the priests as well as the place from where the country was administered in the 20th Dynasty. It was moreover a site with ancient religious traditions as it was said to have been built on the hill where eight primordial divinities that existed prior to the creation of the world were buried and where the god Amun appeared for the first time.

The archaeological area comprises a temple from the 18th Dynasty dedicated to Amun and built during the reign of Thutmosis III, the temple of Rameses III, the chapels of the worshippers of Amun, the small temple of Thot, the site of the royal palace of Amenhotep III, the stores, the sacred lake and nilometer. The whole complex was surrounded by a wall by Rameses III who wanted to render it similar to a fortress.

The temple of Rameses III is the site's most important monument, the Ramesseum being the inspiration for what was one of the most grandiose examples of Theban architecture.

The entrance comprises two massive pylons standing no less than 22 metres high and featuring sculpted military scenes including one of the king striking down with a mace a group of prisoners belonging to the subject peoples of Egypt and one with the pharaoh wearing the double crown and a sword sacrificing prisoners to Amun and another of the pharaoh hunting the wild bull.

**134**

*A view of the south portico
in the first courtyard, with
the large columns covered
with polychrome bas-reliefs.*

**135 left**

*The pilasters of the portico
in the second courtyard are
decorated with scenes of
offerings.*

**135 top right**

*Bas-relief sculpted on the
south-west side of the first
pylon depicting Rameses III
hunting a bull.*

**135 centre right**

*Detail of one of the bas-
relief scenes decorating the
walls of the first courtyard.*

**135 bottom right**

*Polychrome bas-relief with
the winged solar disc, sculpted
on one of the architraves of
the second courtyard.*

In the first great courtyard there is a portico with eight columns on one side and a gallery supported by Osirian pilasters and still decorated with battle scenes and offerings to the gods on the other.

The second pylon features bas reliefs exalting military exploits with an abundance of details. There follows a second courtyard with Osirian pilasters and columns with closed capitals delineating a portico decorated with religious and military bas-reliefs.

From the courtyard one reaches the three hypostyle halls, of which the first had no less than 24 columns, and the inner sanctum that contained the sacred barque of Amun; the sacellum is flanked by the remains of two chapels dedicated to Mut and Khonsu, while a short distance away is the chapel of Ra-Harmachis and that of the deified Rameses III himself. The external walls are all sculpted with bas reliefs that continue to illustrate military exploits such as the naval battle with the sea peoples. An important element for scholars among the reliefs is a calendar listing the various religious festivities. Entering the temple today, one finds the following sequence of elements: a Roman courtyard from the imperial epoch, a Roman colonnade, a pylon from the era of Ptolemy IX and XII, the Nectanebo courtyard and a pylon from the era of Shabaka. The original temple was begun by Amenhotep I and completed by Hatshepsut and Thutmosis III, as shown by certain figures and the cartouches found within the shrine. The consecrated part of the temple was then occupied during the Christian era by the Copts who left writings and paintings.

**136-137**
*Aerial view of Deir al-Bahari, with the grandiose*

*temple of Hatshepsut and the adjacent temples of Thutmosis III and Mentuhotep.*

**136 bottom left**
*In this bas-relief, Queen Hatshepsut, portrayed with*

*male features, is offering a number of votive gifts to the falcon-headed god, Horus.*

*136 bottom right*
*A painted limestone sphinx*
*with the face of Hatshepsut,*
*found at Deir al-Bahari.*

*137 left*
*View of the intermediate*
*portico, better known as the*
*"Portico of Punt".*

*137 top right*
*One of the friezes which best*
*preserves its colours depicts a*
*vulture surmounted by a*
*long series of ureaus.*

*137 bottom right*
*Bas-relief depicting the god*
*Amun-Ra.*

# DEIR AL-BAHARI
# THE TEMPLE OF HATSHEPSUT

Set in a spectacular natural amphitheatre of reddish rock, sacred to the goddess Hathor, stand three temples that, when the sun is high in the sky and the glare is dazzling, blend into the background of rocky walls. This, the so-called Monastery of the North, takes its name from the Coptic monastery built a short distance away of which just a few ruins remain today. The charisma of Queen Hatshepsut has endured over the millennia, earning her a place in the pantheon of great Egyptian sovereigns. Research is still being conducted into her family ties with Thutmosis II and Thutmosis III, while fanciful hypotheses have been put forward regarding her relationship with the architect Senmut. This last was responsible for the construction of what is a highly original temple. Despite being rebuilt, virtually stone by stone, from the ruins first brought to light by Naville in 1891, the building will never match the spectacular magnificence of its past.

Originally, a gently rising monumental avenue led towards the rocky amphitheatre, flanked by sphinxes and surrounded by gardens. The avenue reached a first large courtyard with flower beds and a colonnade interrupted by a second ramp leading to the upper level. The wall of the portico was decorated with bas reliefs on a number of registers with ritual scenes of hunting and fishing and the ceremony of the erection of the obelisks in the temple of Amun at Karnak. The second terrace features two porticoes to the north (unfinished) with 15 columns and 4 niches and a portico with 44 square columns in a double row. To the left is a chapel dedicated to Hathor and to the right another dedicated to Anubis. Important bas-reliefs rich in detail decorate the walls of the portico with scenes from the life of the queen and the famous expedition to the Land of Punt.

Climbing a ramp one reaches the portico of the third terrace with 22 columns preceded by partially reconstructed Osirian pilasters, while a pink granite doorway leads into the hypostyle hall of which just

*138 top left*
*Bas-relief depicting sculpted*
*in the south-western corner*
*of the Portico of Punt,*
*depicting the transportation*
*of incense trees.*

*138 centre left*
*Detail of a bas-relief from*
*the Portico of Punt in*
*which a number of rowers*
*are depicted in action.*

*138 bottom left*
*Detail of a bas-relief from*
*the Portico of Punt.*

*138-139*
*Three of the reconstructed*
*Osiris colossal statues set*
*against the pilasters of the*
*upper portico, representing*
*Queen Hatshepsut.*

a few columns remain. On the left there are the two chapels dedicated to the royal cult of the queen and Thutmosis I while to the right is the one dedicated to the solar cult of Ra-Horakty. At the end of the hall is the entrance to the shrine of Amun where the sacred barque would once have been kept.

On the right of the third terrace is the chapel of Hathor composed of two hypostyle halls and other rooms and niches carved into the mountain and containing interesting bas reliefs and the figure of the architect Senmut which appears a number of times behind the doors of certain niches.

Mention must be made of the deeply excavated tomb of Senmut, located close to the entrance to the first terrace. It contains a portrait of the architect while the ceiling features a representation of the constellations and the months of the year.

The tomb was never finished and Senmut was buried in the necropolis of Sheik Abd-al-Quarna, a fact that has alimented Egyptologists' studies and stimulated speculation about the queen and her vizier.

## THE TEMPLE OF MENTUHOTEP I

The first of the temple to be built at Deir al-Bahari and was the tomb of the first pharaoh of the Theban 11th Dynasty, Mentuhotep I who began the process of the unification of Egypt following the tormented First Intermediate Period.

The layout of the building was inspired by the temples of the Old Kingdom, to the extent that it resembled the funerary complex of Djoser and in part the sun temples of Abu Sir. The texts of the 12th Dynasty called the temple "Akh-Sut-Nebhepetre"

which means "Glorious are the places of Mentuhotep". The burial chamber is found in a subterranean grotto carved into the mountain at a depth of around 45 metres and is accessed via a descending corridor. Another tunnel leads to a crypt built as a cenotaph where Howard Carter discovered a painted sandstone statue that can now be seen in the Museum of Cairo. A pyramid with a base of around 20 metres probably once rose above the main building (mastaba). The design of the building was architecturally innovative both in terms of the access ramp to the terrace with walkways adorned with hexagonal columns forming a portico, and for the large hypostyle hall which was built with no less than 80 columns.

## THE TEMPLE OF THUTMOSIS III

This tomb was discovered relatively recently (1962) as in its ruined state it had actually be overlooked. Bas-reliefs in limestone were discovered along with statues and graffiti left by the worshipers of the goddess Hathor. These relics are now conserved in the museums of Luxor and Cairo. The monument was built in the space between the rear hypostyle of the temple of Mentuhotep and the third terrace of the temple of Hatshepsut and was consecrated to Amun and Hathor. The temple also featured a large hall with 76 columns, a terrace and an access ramp.

*139 bottom left*
*The king and queen of Punt, the latter displaying signs of pathological obesity.*

*139 top right*
*One of the Hathoric capitals that adorn the columns of the chapel of Hathor.*

*139 bottom right*
*Another detail from the decorative scheme of the Portico of Punt, this time featuring two bearers.*

140 top left
Detail of the burial chamber
in the tomb of
Tutankhamun.

140 centre left
The south-east corner of the
vestibule in the tomb of
Horemheb.

# The Theban Necropolises

## THE VALLEY OF THE KINGS

Having left the green banks of the Nile and passed through the colourful villages, the road leads towards the rocky mountains rising behind Deir al-Bahari and penetrates a valley which itself branches into two further narrow and rugged valleys: the Valley of the Kings to the east, also known as the East Valley and identified by the code KV, and the Valley of the Monkeys or West Valley identified by the code WV.

The West Valley is not generally included in tourist itineraries due to the restricted number of tombs (four), only two of which (those of Amenhotep III and Ay) are open to the public. The Valley of the Kings instead houses 58 tombs identified with the KV code followed by the progressive number attributed on their discovery.

The area of Thebes West was conceived and utilised as a necropolis in the First Intermediate Period (2152-1994 BC) when three sovereigns of the Theban 11th Dynasty were buried there, beyond the west bank of the Nile at Al-Tarif. In the Middle Kingdom, the pharaoh Mentuhotep I had his tomb and funerary temple built in the stunning natural amphitheatre of Deir al-Bahari, the remains still being visible alongside the temple of Queen Hatshepsut. The oldest hypogean (subterranean) tombs in the Valley of the Kings appear to be KV 38 (attributed to Thutmosis I and built by the architect Ineni) and KV 20 built at the behest of Hatshepsut for herself and her father Thutmosis I (1504-1492 BC), while the last pharaoh to be buried in the valley was Rameses XI (1104-1075 BC).

140 bottom left
A view of the vestibule of the tomb of Horemheb, with the pharaoh before the gods.

140 right
Another detail of the wall paintings decorating the tomb of Horemheb.

141
The profusely decorated burial chamber of the tomb of Tutankhamun. It contains the magnificent pink quartzite sarcophagus which itself contains the first anthropoid coffin of the sovereign.

**142 bottom right**
The barque of Ra, painted
in the burial chamber of the
tomb of Rameses I.

**143 top**
The burial chamber in the
tomb of Sety I, showing the
astronomical ceiling.

**143 bottom**
The burial chamber in the
tomb of Rameses I, with the
pink granite sarcophagus.

**142-143**
131 A view of the
chamber of four pillars in
the tomb of Sety I.

**142 bottom left**
The Fourth Hour of the
Book of Doors, a wall
painting in the tomb of
Rameses I.

The tombs of the Theban valleys are all
hypogean and of the "syringe-type" as the Greeks
called them. The depth, the extension of the
excavations and the subterranean configuration
varied from tomb to tomb (no two are identical) as
is demostrated by the composition of the tomb of
Tutankhamun (KV 62–just four rooms) compared
to that of Rameses II's children (KV 5–no less than
95). All of the rooms — stairways, corridors, halls
with colonnades, niches and the funerary chamber
— are decorated with bright colours on tinted
backgrounds, according to the fashions of the period
in which they were built. Some of the tombs have
almost perfect frescos, others have been restored
with varying degrees of skill, while still others are
badly damaged and in some cases unfinished.
The latter should not be ignored as they allow us
to observe the techniques of painting and bas-
relief sculpture used by the ancient artists and
understand the stages in the artistic process.

The internal decoration, whilst being
different from one tomb to the next in pictorial
terms, was repetitive in the themes tackled: there
are always scenes of rituals and monotonous

transcriptions of passages from sacred religious texts such as the *Book of the Dead* and the religious works of the New Kingdom. The aim was that of assisting the deceased on his journey through the underworld (*Am-Duat*). There are frequent representations of the solar barque with numerous deities overseeing the pharaoh's journey and protecting him from the evil spirits and the serpent Apophis.

The choice of tombs to visit is not free as the Egyptian authorities open the tombs in rotation so as to reduce the damage caused by the humidity brought in by the visitors. The entrance ticket to the valley generally includes entrance to three tombs (separate tickets can be purchased to visit the other tombs open at that time). It is suggested that you visit the following tombs–three historical groups:

1st Period: KV 34 THUTMOSIS III
 KV 35 AMENHOTEP II
 KV 43 THUTMOSIS IV
2nd Period: KV 57 HOREMHEB
 KV 17 SETY I
 KV 8 MERENPTAH
3rd Period: KV 11 RAMESES III
 KV 9 RAMESESE VI

To this selection may be added the small tomb of Tutankhamun (KV 62) which only features decoration in the burial chamber containing the attractive sarcophagus in pink granite, with a second anthropomorphic sarcophagus in gilded wood containing the mummy of the young pharaoh. All of the funerary furnishings (3,500) found by Howard Carter in 1922 are in the Museum of Cairo.

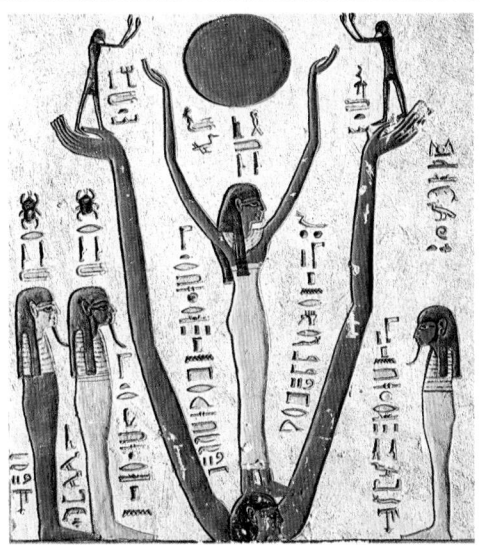

**147 top**
Detail of the burial chamber of
the tomb of Rameses VI: the
solar disc is being lifted into
the sky by the goddess Nut.

**147 bottom**
The burial chamber in the
tomb of Rameses VI
containing the sarcophagus
broken by thieves.

**146-147**
The astronomical ceiling of
the burial chamber in the
tomb of Rameses IX, with
the goddess Nut swallowing
the solar disc.

**146 bottom left**
The magnificent sarcophagus
in red porphyry in the
burial chamber of the tomb
of Rameses IV.

**146 bottom right**
A detail of the complex
decorative scheme adorning
the tomb of Rameses IV.

**148-149**
A view of the Valley of the
Queens, the southernmost of
the Theban necropolises.

**148 bottom left**
The entrance to the tomb of
Meritamun, the daughter
and consort of Rameses II.

**148 bottom right**
One of the rooms in the
tomb of Meritamun.

**149 top**
A detail of the ante-chamber
in the tomb of Amun-her-
khepshef, son of Rameses II.

**149 bottom**
Polychromatic bas-relief in
the burial chamber of the
tomb of Ka-em-uaset.

## THE VALLEY OF THE QUEENS

The Valley of the Queens is quickly reached after passing the Colossi of Memnon, leaving the temple of Medinet-Habu on the right and heading west for around two kilometres.

Today the locality is known as Biban al-Harim but in ancient times it had the more appropriate and attractive name of "Ta-set-Neferu". While the compound place-name is difficult to translate, in the ancient Egyptian language the word *neferu* expressed a

was subsequently abandoned due to the unstable terrain, many others were damaged by the rare but heavy rains, while still others were destroyed by Coptic religious vandals who built a monastery in the area, the ruins of which are still visible.

Despite its name, the valley was used for the burial not only of the queens, but also the sons and daughters of the kings andsome court dignitaries, while in the Roman epoch even commoners were buried here. Research in the valley began following

concept of beauty found in numerous names that are associated in our collective imagination with the perfection of queens such as Nefertiti and Nefertari.

As with the Valley of the Kings, the site chosen for the tombs was protected by the pyramidal mountain al-Qurn and, moreover, according to some authorities, the natural cavern eroded by flood waters at the bottom of the valley might have represented a divine uterus from which the deceased buried in the valley could be reborn. Evidence of around a hundred tombs has been found in the Valley of the Queens. Work on many of these commenced but

the Franco-Tuscan expedition organised by Champollion and Rosellini in 1829, although Belzoni had entered the valley in 1816, leaving graffiti on the entrance to the tomb of Tyti. There followed Lepsius, Brugsch and finally the expedition of 1903 led by Schiapparelli who brought to light all of the most important tombs visible today, including the tomb of Nefertari, Rameses II's "great royal bride", which is considered the best in the valley and one of the greatest of all the Theban tombs. The tombs in this Valley, all from the 18th, 19th, 20th and 21th Dynasties, are identified with the code QV.

**150 and 151**
*All the images on these pages reproduce details of the sumptuous decorative scheme adorning the walls of the tomb of Nefertari, discovered by Ernesto Schiapparelli in 1904 and subjected to a long and complex restoration completed in 1992.*

## THE TOMB OF NEFERTARI (QV 66)

Nefertari (Nofretari-Mery-am-Mut) was the favourite wife of Rameses II: never before in Egypt had a queen been held in such high regard by a pharaoh who, in her honour, ordered the construction of a temple at Abu Simbel alongside his own and the excavation of a tomb worthy of a sovereign. This tomb is the most beautiful and most richly decorated in the Valley of the Queens.

The origins of Nefertari are not absolutely clear. She was probably born into a noble Theban family and may have been related in some way to

Ay, the successor to Tutankhamun in 1323 BC. She married Rameses II before his coronation and had five or six children from him. We also know little about Nefertari's death other than the fact that after the jubilee marking the 30th anniversary of Rameses II's reign, her name no longer appeared in the inscriptions and thus she may have died around 1250 BC at an age of around 40/45 years.

The tomb was discovered by Ernesto Schiapparelli in 1904 during the first systematic search of the Valley of the Queens performed by the Italian Archaeological Mission. It was closed to the public for many years to avoid damaging the paintings with restoration work that began in 1988 being completed in 1992. Since then the subterranean tomb has been reopened but only for a restricted number of visitors which means tickets need to be booked in advance.

The plan of this tomb is more complex than those of the others in the valley and was derived from the examples in the Valley of the Kings. Following the first flight of stairs from the entrance the sequence of rooms is as follows: antechamber, vestibule and annexe, a second flight of steps leading to the burial chamber with two annexes

**152 and 153**
*The tomb of Nefertari,
with its very complex plan
and sumptuous decorative
scheme is considered to be
one of the most beautiful in
the Valley of the Queens. In
order to preserve the
splendour of the delicate
decoration, access to the
tomb has been drastically
restricted.*

and a cell. Specialist texts should be consulted for a
more detailed description, but the following
information may suffice for ordinary visitors.

The ceilings are fairly low compared with those
of other tombs and are all painted a deep blue and
decorated with gold five-pointed stars as seen in a
number of tombs in the Valley of the Kings. The
solid rectangular section pilasters are decorated
with divinities and frequently the *djed* symbol with
the cartouches and titles of the queen. The walls are
in turn decorated with excerpts from the *Book of the
Dead*, with texts and figures illustrating the journey
of the queen's spirit as she descends to the
underworld before being reborn as a deity.

*154 top left*
The interior of the Ptolemaic
temple at Deir al-Medina.

*154 bottom left*
The restored interior of the
same tomb.

*154 centre left*
The entrance to the tomb of
Ipui at Deir al-Medina.

*154 right*
A view of the workers'
village of Deir al-Medina.

## THE SITE OF DEIR AL-MEDINA

Deir al-Medina is close to the Valley of the
Queens and less than 2 kilometres from the
Valley of the Kings. It was from here that the
footpaths followed by the workers excavating and
decorating the royal tombs departed.

Today we find the remains of the workers'
village, the tombs of the craftsmen cut into the
mountainside and a small temple from the
Ptolemaic era dedicated to Hathor-Maat and later
used by Coptic Christians as a monastery.
Founded and inhabited from the 18th Dynasty
onwards, when works began in the Valley of the
Kings with the tomb of Thutmosis I, the village
has a rectangular plan and occupies a surface area
of around 6,500 square metres. At the height of
its expansion it could accommodate around 700
people.

Local excavations have brought to light the
foundations of houses, the layout of the streets
and a wealth of relics that have allowed, a
relatively rare occurrence, the everyday lives of
ordinary families to be reconstructed.

The necropolis of Deir al-Medina was built
on the slopes of the hill overlooking the village to
the west and comprises over 400 tombs from the
19th and 20th Dynasties, of which only 53 are
frescoed.

The local tombs typically feature an imposing
entrance with pylons similar to a miniature
temple, an internal courtyard leading to the
chapel and a shaft or a steep flight of steps down
to the funerary chamber cut into the rock. The
chapels were frequently surmounted externally by
a small pyramid in unfired bricks.

The interiors and, in particular, the burial
chambers, were richly frescoed in bright colours,

**154-155**
A panoramic view of the
temple of Deir al-Medina,
surrounded by a high brick
enclosure wall.

**155 bottom left**
A view of the necropolis of
Deir al-Medina, with the
characteristic pyramid
entrance to one of the tombs.

**155 bottom right**
The interior of the tomb of
Khabekhnet, a functionary
at the time of Rameses II,
with the two fragmentary

statuary groups representing
the deceased's parents (to the
left of the door) and the
deceased himself with his
consort (right).

*156 top left*

The north-east wall of the
tomb of Sennegem, on which
the sacred Fields of Iaru, in
the underworld, are depicted.

*156 bottom left*

A view of the sumptuous
interior of the tomb of
Pashedu, with a scene where
he is drinking at a spring.

while the funerary chambers and annexes
contained furnishings, objects and foods for the
underworld.

The most tombs of greatest interest are the
following.

## Senegem (TT I)

A necropolis functionary at the time of Sety I
and Rameses II, Senegem's tomb is frescoed on
an ochre ground with scenes of religious
ceremonies and everyday life in excellent
condition. The tomb was found virtually intact
and all the furnishings are conserved in the
Museum of Cairo.

## Pashedu (TT 3)

Necropolis functionary and chief painter of
the tomb of Sety I.

## Ipuy (TT 217)

Chief sculptor of the necropolis, Ipuy's house
in the village has also been identified. The tomb
features interesting scenes depicting everyday life
(agriculture, trade, boat-building, weaving and
so on).

## Inherkhaon (TT 359)

Inherkhaon was defined as "foreman of the
lord of the two lands in the plaza of truth" and
worked for Rameses II and IV during the 20th
Dynasty.

The crypt is composed of two vaulted
chambers brightly painted with figures from the
*Book of the Dead*.

**156 right**
*The wife of Pashedu, Negemtebehdet, portrayed in the style typical of the Ramesside Period.*

**156-157**
*The magnificent interior of the tomb of Sennegem, a functionary who lived at the time of Sety I: portrayed on*

*the back wall are the deceased and his wife Inyferti worshipping the gods of the underworld, overlooked by two images of Anubis.*

**158 top**
The entrance to the monumental tomb of Ramose, a high ranking dignitary at the time of Amenhotep IV.

**158 bottom**
Preparatory drawing for a never completed painting in the tomb of Ramose.

**158 top centre**
The interior of the hypostyle hall of the tomb of Ramose, which featured no less than 32 compound columns.

**158 bottom centre**
A detail of a wall painting in the tomb of Ramose.

# THE NECROPOLIS OF SHEIKH ABD-EL-QURNA

Between Deir al-Medina and the hilly area to the west of the temple of Sety I lie over 500 tombs of high ranking functionaries and notables from the 18th Dynasty (the Tombs of the Nobles), grouped in a number of necropolises named according to their locations. The most representative site is that of Sheikh Abd-el-Qurna, located on a terrace between Deir al-Medina and Deir al-Bahari and comprising many well preserved tombs. The local tombs are not very large and are generally composed of an open courtyard, a vestibule in which the titles of the deceased are found, and a corridor leading to the burial chamber with niches. These tombs feature more down-to-earth and subjects than the religious symbolism of the royal tombs in the Valley of the Kings, a difference similar to that between the images in the mastabas and those typical of the funerary monuments of the Old Kingdom. The paintings boast magnificent colours and are extremely attractive, but are also remarkable for the joyful serenity with which life is represented within a funerary setting. Only around thirty of the tombs are open to visitors and an inevitable selection should be made from among the following:

Sennefer (TT 96): mayor of the City of the South (Amenhotep II)

Khaemhat (TT 57): Royal Scribe and Inspector of the Granaries (Amenhotep III)

Khonsu (TT 31): First Prophet of Men-kheper-ra (Thutmosis I)

Rekhmire (TT 100): Vizier and Governor of the City (Thutmosis III - Amenhotep II)

Menna (TT 69): Scribe of the Land Register (Thutmosis IV)

Nakht (TT 52): Scribe-astronomer of Amun (Thutmosis IV)

Paser (TT 106): Vizier and Governor of the Valley (Sety I - Rameses II)

Haremhab (TT 78): Royal Scribe (Thutmosis III - Amenhotep III)

Kenamon (TT 93): Chief Intendent to the King (Amenhotep III)

Ramose (TT 55): Vizier and Governor of the City (Amenhotep IV)

**158-159**
A detail of the interior of the tomb of Panehesi.

**159 bottom left**
A view of the sumptuous tomb of Neferronpet.

**159 bottom right**
View of the somptuous tomb of Neferronpet.

# Esna

Esna is located 58 kilometres to the south of Luxor, on the left bank of the Nile and over the ruins of the city of Latopolis. It was a prosperous trading centre during the New Kingdom thanks to its geographical position at the convergence of the roads linking the Nile valley with the cities of the south.

The principal deity venerated at Esna was the ram-headed god Khnum, a creator who modelled every animal and plant on his potter's wheel. The Temple of Esna is dedicated to this divinity and the goddess Neith who was represented as a lates fish (*latus niloticus*, hence the name Latopolis). The temple—transformed in to a Christian church and lastly used as a store for cotton in more recent times—was discovered by Champollion in 1828, and was actually a reconstruction from the reign of Ptolemy VI in the 1st century AD, of a building from the 18th Dynasty. It is located in the heart of the city, below street level. All that remains of the temple built during the reigns of Tiberius, Claudius and Vespasian is a large hypostyle hall measuring 33 by 16.5 metres, with 24 columns

**160 top left**
*A view of the interior of the large hypostyle hall, the ceiling of which is supported by 18 columns.*

**160 bottom left**
*The cross-pieces that link the columns of the facade are profusely decorated with bas-reliefs.*

**161 top right**
This bas-relief on one of the
internal columns shows the
emperor Trajan offering
lotus flowers to the god
Khnum.

**161 bottom right**
The capitals inside the
hypostyle hall are
characterised by a lively
colour scheme.

**160-161**
*The large hypostyle hall—an
excellent example of the
religious architecture of the
Ptolemaic Period—is all that
remains of the temple
consecrated to the ram-
headed god, Khnum.*

with magnificent capitals decorated with floral
motifs. The last hieroglyphs to be carved in the
temple date from the middle of the 3rd century AD,
as do the mural decorations with symbolic images
of the fraticidal struggle between the Roman
emperors. Linked to those of the ceiling depicting
the zodiac, the constellations and the course of the
sun underline the concept that the entire universe is
enclosed within the temple and that it was built in
accordance with the laws of the cosmos.

The back wall features two unusual inscriptions,
hymns to the god Khnum. The first is composed
exclusively of the hieroglyphic symbol of the
crocodile, the second of the hieroglyphic symbol of
the ram.

**162 top**
The statue of Horus in the
form of a falcon set before the
entrance to the hypostyle hall.

**162 bottom**
The facade of the first
hypostyle hall features six
columns united at the bottom
by decorated cross-pieces.

**162-163**
The temple of Edfu, of
which the 47-metre high
entrance pylon is seen here,
is considered to be one of the
best preserved in all Egypt.

**163 bottom left**
One of the bas-reliefs
decorating the peripheral
corridor shows the pharaoh
receiving the double crown.

**163 bottom right**
The replica of the solar boat
built by Mariette in the late
19th century is conserved in
one of the internal halls.

# Edfu

E dfu, known to the ancients as Hebau, is
situated around 100 kilometres south of
Luxor, on the west bank of the Nile. It was the
capital of the second *nome* of Upper Egypt, an
important and wealthy city since the Old Kingdom

and the home of to Horus, the celestial god
represented by the falcon whose wings symbolise
the extension of the cosmos. The temple dedicated
to this deity is remarkably well preserved, probably
thanks to the long period during which it was
buried beneath the desert sands. Only the upper
parts of the building allowed the French expedition
of 1798 to identify the site and it was not until
1860 that Auguste Mariette, then the director of
the Service des Antiquités Egyptiennes, began work
to free it from the sands.

The building as we see it today is virtually
intact and in terms of size is the second largest
Egyptian temple after Karnak and the largest of the
monuments dedicated to Horus. Work on the
temple began in 237 BC during the reign of Ptolemy

III and was finished in 57 BC, under Ptolemy XII.

The temple is entered via the monumental
portal set between the two towers of the pylon.
Above this portal is a balcony from which once a
year during a solemn ritual, the priests presented the
falcon chosen to embody the living god (to this end
a school of falconry was established at Edfu).

Having passed the two towers, one enters a
courtyard bound on three sides by a colonnade,
with the entrance to the first hypostyle hall at the
far end. This hall contains one of the most
imposing statues of Horus ever sculpted, while at
the sides are two small chambers, the House of the
Morning celebrates rising of the sun and symbolises
the faith required to enter to the temple, and the
House of Books on the left which gave access to
sacred knowledge. Beyond the first hall is a second,
smaller hypostyle hall with 12 columns which in
turn communicates with three chambers, the first
on the right is the so-called "treasure chamber" and
conserves the names of the mineral-rich regions
annexed by Egypt, while on the left is the room of
the Nile bringing prosperity and the Laboratory
with inscribed recipes for perfumes and unguents
used in religious ceremonies.

The second hall leads to the offerings chamber
and is linked via a roof to a central chamber. On the
left of this last is a chapel dedicated to the god Min,
while to the right is a small courtyard with an altar
and chapel used as a vestibule.

Inside the central chamber or *naos* is the true

inner sanctum, a temple within a temple containing an altar housing a statue of the god, surrounded by a corridor with chapels in which scenes of the Horus legend are inscribed.

Daily worship took the form of three services, one in the morning with offerings of food by the priest who entered the *naos* and, in the presence of the statue, fed its power before closing the door of the *naos* and eliminating evidence of his passing by walking backwards; the second was at midday, the *naos* remained closed but aspersions and fumigations were performed. The last service held in the evening, consisted of a ritual of offerings and purification through incense. At Edfu can be seen a typical feature of temple architecture, the symbolic succession of spaces that are ever smaller and darker.

# Kom Ombo

**K**om Ombo, or the city of gold, known to the ancient Greeks and Egyptians as Ombos and Nubit respectively, is situated on the right bank of the Nile, around 50 kilometres from Aswan. Thanks to its strategic position above a promontory from which it was easy to survey the river traffic, Kom Ombo became a site of primary importance for the Egyptian army, allowing it to set a second stronghold on the Nile after Aswan.

The city nonetheless remained essentially a centre of agriculture and trade with Nubia, above all throughout the Ptolemaic Period. Building work on the temple began during the reign of Ptolemy VI, was completed under Ptolemy XII and was based on the remains of a shrine dating back to the 18th Dynasty and brought to light during excavations conducted in 1893.

The building is dedicated to two deities, Sobek the crocodile god and Haroeris (Horuis the Elder), the falcon god; in this case Sobek is identified as the evil Seth, the enemy of Horus. The temple features a great number of crocodiles as the Egyptians believed that by transforming them into religious icons they would be spared by the fearsome reptiles. Many examples were kept in

*164 top*
*The remains of a portal erected at the behest of Ptolemy XII stand alongside the temple.*

*164 centre*
*One of the bas-reliefs decorating the rooms at the back of the temple.*

captivity and mummified on their death.

Of the Ptolemaic temple, only part of the curtain wall, a number of columns, a few sections of the *pronao* and the chapels and a *mammisi* have survived. The entrance is constituted by the pylon forming part of the monumental portal, with twin doors for Sobek and Horus of which little remains. To the south of the great courtyard, on the right of the temple, is a chapel dedicated to the goddess Hathor containing numerous crocodile mummies. Beyond the pylon lies the courtyard delimited by now ruined colonnades and featuring a sacrificial altar in the centre. From here one reaches the first of the hypostyle halls with twin entrances which had function of purifying the pharaoh by both Horus and Thot in the presence of the temple deities Sobek and Haroeris.

The two conflicting deities are obliged to co-operate in the struggle against the forces of darkness. This dualism is also seen in the architectural layout, with the following arrangement of the elements making the complex: two entrances, two corridors surrounding the *naos*, dual passages between the various parts of the building and the inner sanctum divided into two shrines. In the context of this dualism the two deities are consecrated not so much separately as integrated parts of each other. The second hypostyle hall, smaller than the first, boasts walls decorated with numerous hieroglyphs concerning the rules and conduction of rituals

*164 bottom*
*Another of the bas-reliefs decorating the rooms located behind the shrines in which the pharaoh is shown making offerings to various divinities.*

*164-165*
*Lateral view of the remains of the first and second hypostyle halls, preceded by what remains of the double porticoed courtyard.*

*165 bottom*
*The front of the well
preserved chapel of Hathor,
erected by the*

*emperor Domitian, in
which the mummies of the
sacred crocodiles are
conserved.*

with the respective places and dates. Three halls
anticipate the inner sanctum. In the first, the
pharaoh lays the foundations of the temple, the
second, known as the Hall of Offerings, gives access
to the roof where at the beginning of each year the
ritual of union with the solar disc was celebrated;
during this ritual the statues of the deities (kept in
the third hall) were exposed to the light of the new
year in order to absorb positive energy. At the heart
of the three halls lies the inner sanctum, probably
once divided into two parts separated by a wall,
with on the left the area dedicated to Haroeris and
on the right, that of Sobek.

**166-167**
*The course of the Nile, seen from Elephantine Island.*

**166 bottom left**
*The celebrated Nilometer, on Elephantine Island.*

**166 bottom centre**
*One of the inscribed boulders on Elephantine Island.*

**166 bottom right**
*The Broken Obelisk that lies in a quarry at Aswan.*

# Aswan

A swan, known in ancient times as Syene, is situated in an enchanting natural setting that makes it one of the most inviting attractions in the whole of Egypt. The lush vegetation mitigates the high temperatures brought by the warm winds from the desert, whilst the Nile, here divided by Elephantine Island, seems more blue than further down the valley. A point of departure fort visits to the Nubian temples, Aswan offers a number of archaeological attractions including the ruins on the Island of Elephantine, once the capital of the first and southernmost *nome* of Egypt. Here, in the welcome shade of sycamore tree, is the entrance to the famous Nilometer, partially rebuilt in the Roman epoch and carrying inscriptions dating from the reigns of Thutmosis III, Amenhotep III (18th Dynasty) and Psamtek II (26th Dynasty). In all probability, however, its construction dates back to even earlier times; it was partially rebuilt during the Roman era. Still on the island, further excavations have brought to light a late temple of Khnum (30th Dynasty) and the temple of Satet, his female counterpart (18th Dynasty). On the southern tip of the island is a Ptolemaic temple rebuilt using blocks of stone belonging to the foundations of the temple of Kalabsha. Crossing the river by felucca and landing on the western bank, one may visit the subterranean tombs dug into the mountains by the princes of Elephantine, their long, steep access stairs visible from the town. There are notable tombs belonging to Sirenput I and Sirenput II, both the first superintendent of the priests of Khnum and Satet and governor of Aswan. Following a rapid visit to the Christian monastery St. Simeone, established in the 7th century and rebuilt in the 10th century, the quarries to the north of the city, where the Egyptians extracted rock for their monumental buildings and obelisks are undoubtedly worthy of close inspection. An unfinished example of the latter was abandoned in the quarry after the stone cracked. Nearby a museum houses relics mainly found in Nubia.

*167 top*
*One of the decorated boulders on the island of Sehel.*

*167 centre*
*The remains of the temple of Satet on Elephantine Island.*

*167 bottom*
*The small obelisk from Abu Simbel, now at the entrance to the Elephantine Island archaeological museum.*

# *Philae*

Situated to the south of Aswan, the monumental complex of Philae features the largest of the temples dedicated to Isis. Built during the 3rd century BC, this was the last bastion of ancient Egyptian religion, the place in which the last hieroglyphs were inscribed, in 437 AD. It long remained the only temple in which the Egyptian priests could still perform the old rites in a period in which Christianity was spreading. In 535 the Roman emperor Justinian had the temple closed definitively; the scribes and the priests were exiled, the doors to the inner sanctum were forced and the temple fell into the hands of the Christian hermits who devastated it. The *naos* was profaned and the hypostyle hall became a Christian church.

The need for a reservoir to meet the demand for irrigation water during the seasons in which the Nile is at its lowest led to the construction in the late 19th century of the first dam at Aswan. This was little short of disastrous for the ancient monuments which were thus submerged for much of the year. Then, in 1960, a new threat appeared in the form of work on the construction of a second dam (that created Lake Nasser). On completion of the Aswan High Dam the temple complex would have been permanently submerged to a depth of 4 metres.

Between 1972 and 1980 the buildings at Philae were saved in a remarkable operation involving their transfer to the nearby island of Agilka. Each individual stone was numbered and its position noted so as to allow a faithful reconstruction of the monuments. The operation lasted almost 10 years and in 1980 Philae (or rather the transformed Agilka) was finally reopened to the public.

In antiquity the region represented the interface between the Egyptians and the Nubian peoples. This explains the presence at Philae of shrines

*168 bottom*
The gateway to the Abaton, rebuilt by Ptolemy III on the island of Biga.

*168-169*
The landing place, on Biga, near which are the kiosk and the obelisk of Nectanebo.

*169 bottom*
The Kiosk of Trajan; erected by the Roman emperor in 105 AD.

dedicated to certain deities. During the centuries preceding the expansion of Christianity, the cult of the goddess Isis enjoyed unrivalled popularity that went well beyond the Egyptian borders and was to lead, particularly during the first centuries of the present era, to the erection of sacred buildings dedicated to the goddess in the Roman empire.

The Philae complex is a group of temples, the largest of which is dedicated to the goddess Isis and characterised by an apparent disorder in the elements of which it is composed. Each is set on its own axis and has its own direction, the colonnades are not

parallel but each section has its raison d'être. Isis is the goddess that embodied life itself, and as life is not rational, neither is it symmetrical or parallel.

The landing on the island is to the south, alongside the pavilion of Nectanebo I. From here one passes through two portals opening in a "V" and giving access to the temple of Isis. On the east side of the island is the kiosk of Trajan (rebuilt by the emperor with reliefs illustrating him making offerings to the gods) which housed the barque of Isis used during the processions. Still on the east side, close to the principal temple is the small temple dedicated to the goddess Hathor.

A large paved area precedes the first pylon of the temple of Isis with two tall blocks either side of a small doorway. Having passed the first pylon, one enters a large courtyard, on the west side of which is a free-standing building, the *mammisi*, a temple symbolising the parturition in which Isis gave birth to her son Horus. The east side is instead occupied by a portico housing six small chambers.

The second pylon gives access to the closed area of the temple, behind which is a hall with ten columns. This is a cosmic site, with mythical and astrological decoration linked to the laws of the sky of Isis. Understanding of the rules of sacred astrology was an indispensable condition for access to the twelve-roomed *naos* (each one representing a zodiac sign). The temple also features a crypt and, on the roof, a chapel for the veneration of the god Osiris (Isis's consort), with scenes of the ritual in which Osiris is dead and the king intervenes with the deities to allow the god's spirit to continue to live. Osiris is revived, darkness and death are defeated and the love and faith of Isis triumph over destiny.

In front of the island of Philae lies that of Biga which housed the Abaton, the tomb of Osiris. Today little remains of the temple which once stood there.

*170-171*
The gateway that opens in the first pylon, preceded by two lions installed during the late Roman Period.

*170 bottom*
In the Roman Period the Diocletian gateway was the main entrance to the island.

*171 top*
A view of the kiosk of Nectanebo, with the Hathoric capitals to its columns, and the neighbouring obelisk.

*171 centre*
A perspective view of the eastern colonnade, much of which remains unfinished.

*171 bottom*
The bas-reliefs sculpted on the first pylon show the goddess Isis and the god Horus, the features of which were unfortunately partially obliterated by Coptic monks when the temple was transformed into a Christian church.

# The Nubian Temples

W adi as-Sebua, Amada, Derr, Quertassi... Ancient monuments unknown to modern travellers until recently and four of the eleven archaeological sites in lower Nubia (the ancient Wawat) to survive the inundation caused by the construction of the new dam at Aswan.

Fortunately, many other sites were excavated and examined before the water submerged them for ever, and the most important were dismantled and reconstructed on alternative sites safe from the rising tide. Only in recent years has the introduction of cruises to the region allowed hundreds of visitors to view the monuments each day.

## New Kalabsha, Qertassi, Beit al-Wali

Three temples have been grouped not far from the Philae complex, in the New Kalabsha area around a kilometre south of the Aswan High Dam. They were originally situated within a radius of 50 kilometres from the present site.

The Kalabsha temple, defined by Maspero as "the most beautiful in Nubia", was rebuilt in the age of Augustus in the Ptolemaic style and was consecrated to the cult of deity Mandulis, the Nubian version of the Egyptian god Horus. It is composed of a pylon, a courtyard with porticoes on three sides, a hypostyle hall with twelve columns, two vestibules and a shrine. The transfer from the original site brought to light pre-existing structures from the periods of Amenhotep II and Ptolemy IX. The unfinished temple has a number of interesting features such as depictions of Augustus in the guise of a pharaoh, making offerings to Egyptian deities, and Greek inscriptions relating to the Nubian king Silko who, in the 5th century BC, commemorated his victory of the rival desert tribes. Close to the site is the kiosk of Kertassi, composed of four intact columns clearly dating from the Ptolemaic Period.

## Wadi as-Sebua, Dakka and Maharraka

A desolate, arid, desert land, enclosed by granite mountains dusted with a red sand that at times takes on yellowish tones. This is the panorama that divides New Kalabsha from the second Nubian temple site, around 110 kilometres away, a day's journey by boat. During this silent voyage one passes over the temple of Gerf Hussein, now completely submerged by the

*172 top*
*The elegant and minute kiosk of Kardassy, reconstructed near the temple of Kalabsha.*

*172 centre*
*The small rock temple of Beith al-Whali, also rebuilt at New Kalabsha.*

*172 bottom*
*The innermost hall of the rock temple of Beith al-Whali, supported by massive protodoric columns.*

water. Internally the monument was similar to the temple at Abu Simbel but could not be saved due to the friable nature of the rock from which it had been carved.

One lands at New Sebua where one may admire the temples of Al Dakka, Maharraka and Wadi as-Sebua. This last name, which means in Arabic the "valley of the lions", derives from the sphinxes that adorn the entrance to the temple. The building was erected at the behest of Rameses II and dedicated to the veneration of the god Amun Horakty. The interior features depictions of offerings that were continuously made to the deities in these religious sanctuaries. This site too was restored by the The Copts who transformed it into a Christian church. There is an interesting depiction of St Peter offering flowers to the "powerful bull, king of Upper and Lower Egypt", Ramses II. The complex was moved just 6 kilometres from its original site, with the sphinxes already partially submerged in a desperate race against time.

The temple of Daklla, originally situated 40 kilometres to the north of its present position, dates from the Ptolemaic and Roman Periods. Dedicated to Thot, the temple was built by Ptolemy IV and Arqamani, King of Meroe (circa 200 BC), part of the site covering the remains of older buildings. Further additions were made by Ptolemy VIII and the Roman emperor, Augustus.

In the vicinity of Dakka is Maharaqq, the third temple in the group, located around 30 kilometres from its original position. Of reduced dimensions, and unfinished, the temple was dedicated to the cult of the Ptolemaic god, Serapis.

*172-173*
*The facade of the hypostyle hall in the temple of Kalabsha. This complex consecrated to the god Mandulis was built during the Ptolemaic Period and is considered to be the most grandiose Nubian monument after Abu Simbel.*

*174 top left*
*The Osiris pylon that delimit the long sides of the courtyard in the temple of Wadi Sabua.*

*174 left centre top*
*The temple of Amada, begun by Thutmosis III and completed by Amenhotep II.*

*174 left centre bottom*
*The well conserved pylon of the temple of Dakke.*

## AMADA, DERR AND TOMB OF PENNIUT I

The third site is around 50 kilometres away at Amada, the name being taken from that of the oldest of the structures rebuilt here, the temple of Amada, dedicated to Amun and Ra-Horakty. Built by the Thutmosis III (18th Dynasty) and subsequently extended by Thutmosis IV, during the Amarnian Period, the temple was dedicated to the cult of Amun before being restored to the traditional deities under Sety I. It was later transformed into a Christian church by the Copts. The coloured relief sculptures complicated the removal operation. 3 kilometres of rails were laid on which the temple, fixed to steel frames, was transported to the present site, overcoming a difference in height of over 60 metres.

The temple of Derr, completely carved out of the rock, was dedicated to the cult of Ra-Horakty and was built at the behest of Rameses II. It was rebuilt 11 kilometres from its original site.

The rock tomb of Penniut I, built by a local governor during the reign of Rameses VI completes the site.

*174 bottom left*
*The "Feasting Hall" in the underground temple at al-Derr.*

*174 right*
*One of the sphinxes of the dromos at Wadi Sabua.*

*174-175*
*The splendid temple of Wadi Sabua, preceded by the avenue of sphinxes.*

## QASR IBRIM

The city-fortress of Qasr Ibrim, once set around 60 metres above the level of the Nile, now has to cope with the waters of the lake lapping its foundations. Built by the Nubians following the withdrawal towards Egypt in around 900 BC, it was restored on a number of occasions and extended by the Romans. Subsequently inhabited by the Copts, it was occupied by the Mamlukes fleeing from Ishmael Pasha in 1812. Having captured the fortress, the son of Muhammad 'Ali Pasha destroyed it almost completely.

In 1995 the Supreme Council of Antiquities closed the building to the public and it can now only be admired from the deck of a boat.

*175 top right*
*A view of the courtyard in front of the underground section of the temple of al-Derr.*

*175 bottom right*
*What remains of the fortress of Qasr Ibrim, built during the Roman Period.*

*177 top*
*The cult of Rameses II
triumphed at Abu Simbel.*

*177 bottom*
*Each colossus is around 21
metres tall.*

# Abu Simbel

A round 20 kilometres from Sudanese
territory is one of the most well known
of the Nubian sites, the great temple of Rameses II
and the one dedicated to his beloved wife, Nefertari.

Towards the late 1960s, thanks to a remarkable
engineering project, the temples were cut into
blocks and rebuilt 65 metres higher up, set
between two artificial hills and carefully
positioned maintaining the original orientation, a
condition indispensable to allow, as the pharaoh's
architects intended, the sun's rays to penetrate the
temple's inner chamber twice a year, bathing the
four divinities, Ptah of Memphis, Amun-Ra of
Thebes, Re-Horakty of Heliopolis and the
deified Rameses II himself, in its warm light.

The temple was "rediscovered" early in
the 19th century by the Swiss explorer and
traveller, J.L. Burckhardt, the first
European since the Classical period to
visit the site. To do so, he disguised
himself as an Arab. A few years
later, the Italian G.B. Belzoni
managed to free the entrance to
the temple from the sand,
opening the way for the
visits of many travellers
including celebrities such
as the emperor
Maximillian of Bavaria
and Gustave Flaubert
who, accompanied by
the photographer,
Maxime du Camp,
left us with valuable
images of the temple
facade, still partially

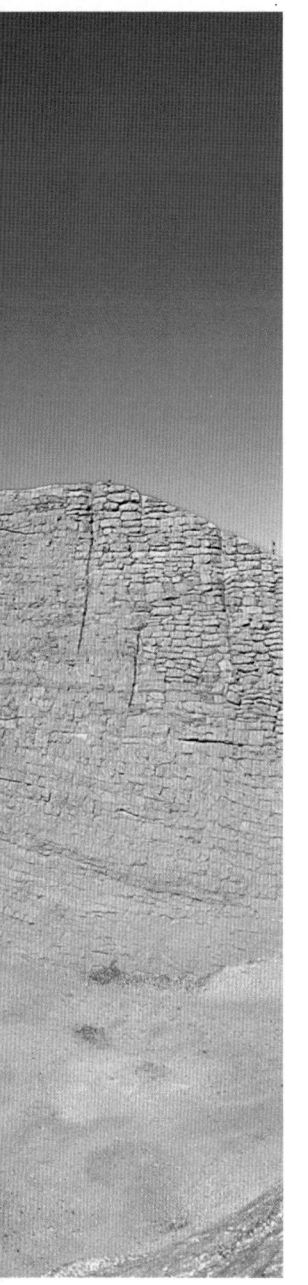

*176-177*
*Panoramic view of Abu
Simbel, in its new setting on
the banks of Lake Nasser.*

*176 bottom left*
*The facade of the main
temple, with the four colossal
statues of Rameses II.*

*176 bottom right*
*Either side of the statues of
the pharaoh are represented
his wife, his mother and his
children to a much smaller
scale.*

**178-179**
*Rameses II dedicated the smaller temple at Abu Simbel to the goddess Hathor and his favourite wife, Nefertari.*

**178 bottom**
*Rameses II had himself represented no less than four times on the facade of his wife's temple.*

buried in the sand.

The temple was principally dedicated to Re-Horakty and originally featured four colossal statues of Rameses II observing the borders of Egypt with placid serenity. One of these collapsed, probably not long after its erection due to an earthquake. Entering the first hall of the temple, one encounters a central nave flanked by Osirian pillars that recall the second courtyard of the Ramesseum. There follows a second, smaller hypostyle hall at the end of which are three chapels. The larger central one houses the four statues of the divinities.

The main theme in the temple decoration is the battle fought by Rameses II against the Hittites at Qadesh, an ancient town in Syria. Excavations and archaeological discoveries in the Hittite sites have greatly revised opinions regarding the king victory, to the point where a rapid withdrawal of the Egyptian troops in the face of an efficient enemy ambush has even been hypothesised.

The smaller temple at Abu Simbel was dedicated to the goddess Hathor and Queen Nefertari, principal and beloved bride of the pharaoh. The facade of the small building features four statues of the king alternating with two of the queen in the guise of the goddess Hathor. Alongside them are the princes and princesses, sons and daughters of the great royal couple. Inside the temple, a single hypostyle hall is divided into three naves, each with six Hathoric pillars. There follows a small vestibule and a small shrine with Hathor in the form of a cow emerging from the rock wall to protect the pharaoh.

**180 top left**
*The four statues carved into the living rock of the shrine in the principal temple: side-by-side from left to right they represent Ptah, Amun-Ra, the deified Rameses II and Ra-Harakhti.*

**180 centre left**
*In the principal temple a bas-relief shows the pharaoh striking down his enemies.*

**180 bottom left**
*The celebrated relief with Rameses on a war chariot.*

**180 right**
*The pillars supporting the ceiling of the hypostyle hall in the smaller temple are decorated with effigies of the goddess Hathor.*

**181**
*The eight Osiris pillars of the principal temple's pronaos that reproduce the features of Rameses II are no less than 10 metres tall.*

*182 top*
The temple of Serabit
al-Khadem is consecrated
to the goddess Hathor.

*182 centre*
A suggestive image of the
site, with a Hathoric stela
in the foreground.

*182 bottom*
A rough bas-relief in which
Hathor is portrayed in the
act of extending the ankh
or "cross of life".

# Serabit al-Khadem

Visiting the temple of Sarabit al-Khadem is not as simple and straightforward as a tourist fresh from visits to the temples of the fertile Nile valley might imagine. This site, built close to a number of turquoise, copper and malachite mines, can in fact only be reached via a thirty-kilometre asphalted road from the coast and a twelve-kilometre drive aboard four-wheel drive vehicles along an unsurfaced track.

There is then an hour's trek to the top of the mountain from which the ancient temple overlooks the valley. Built during the Old Kingdom to offer spiritual protection to the workers in the various mines, and thus dedicated to the goddess Hathor in her manifestation as the "Lady of Turquoise", the Temple of Sarabit al-Khadem performed its task over the following centuries and was embellished with a number of stelae and *ex-votos* during the Middle and New Kingdoms.

Among the relics from the 18th Dynasty are the stelae of Thutmosis III and his co-ruler Queen Hatshepsut. Once Thutmosis was sole sovereign, he took Egyptian expansionism to its extreme, conquering and consolidating positions in foreign lands from which, as in this case, raw materials for religious, military and civil purposes were extracted. Close to the main building, a second temple was later built and dedicated to Sopdu, a deity of the eastern desert.

In spite of the destruction caused by attempts to reopen a number of mines towards the middle of the 19th century, numerous fine stelae and bas-reliefs can still be seen at Sarabit al-Khadem. The turquoises that were mined here were taken along the valley of the Wadi Mattala

*182-183*
The temple of Serabit
al-Khadem is surrounded
by lots of votive stelae
dating to the Middle and
New Kingdom.

*183 bottom*
A view of the small rock
temple consecrated to
Hathor, here defined as the
"Lady of Turquoise".

to the fortified port of Al-Markha (a few kilometres to the south of Abu Zenima) before being shipped to the green valley of the Nile.

A mineral much sought-after by the ancient Egyptians, it was used in the production of necklaces and amulets and in powdered form as a pigment.

**184-185**
A panoramic view of
St. Catherine's monastery,
enclosed by powerful curtain
walls.

**184 bottom left**
A view of the oasis that
extends in the vicinity of the
monastery, irrigated by a
perennial spring.

**184 bottom right**
The campanile of the church
of the Transfiguration rises
alongside the minaret of the
small mosque.

# —— St. Catherine ——

St. Catherine's Monastery stands at an altitude of 1,570 metres in a valley at the foot of Gebel Musa, the Mountain of Moses, traditionally accepted as Mount Sinai. The fortress-monastery was built at the behest of Justinian between 527 and 547 AD to protect the hermits who had settled in this mountainous region of the Sinai from the attacks of the nomadic herders. Since then, on up to the present day, the complex has enjoyed an unusual status. It was spared the consequences of invasions, even during the most intense period of Muslim domination of the area.

Today, just as in the past, the monks that administer the monastery—very hospitable but subject to severe regulations—are of Greek and Cypriot origins. Inside the irregular quadrilateral of the enclosure walls, partly dating back to the Byzantine era, are crowded buildings constructed during the long history of the monastery and they include a minaret which symbolises the unusual tolerance that characterises the institution. The buildingss hugging the enclosure walls, partly used for the monks' and visitors' accommodation and administrative functions, also contain the library—

rich in manuscript codexes, but closed to the public—and the museum, which houses precious icons dating from the 7th to the 18th centuries. The functional structures gravitate around the church of the Transfiguration, a three-naved basilica that contains a precious Cretan iconostasis from the 17th century and the remains of St. Catherine. The parts of the complex associated with the oldest traditions are the biblical well "of Moses" or "of Jethro", and the Chapel of the Burning Bush where an ancient shrub marks the spit in which the prophet is said to have spoken with Yahweh. Near the monastery begins the path to Gebel Musa, a steep, partially stepped track that leads, through the "Confession Gate", to the peak on which Moses is said to have received the Tablets of the Law, today occupied by two recent small buildings: a chapel and a mosque.

**186**
*The central nave of the church of the Transfiguration, with the incredibly rich iconostasis.*

**187 top**
*One of the interiors of the monastic complex.*

**187 centre**
*On top of Gebel Musa is the chapel of the Holy Trinity .*

**187 bottom left**
*The chapel was built in 1934 on foundations from the era of Justinian.*

**187 bottom right**
*The summit of Mount Sinai (2,285 metres) can be reached via a steep flight of over 3,000 steps passing below the celebrated Confession Gate.*

# Glossary

**Abaton:** "inaccessible", indicates a subterranean area of a temple.

**Amarna, Tell al-:** modern name for the location of Akhenaten, "The Horizon of Aten", the new capital founded by Amenhotep IV-Akhenaten (1350-1333 BC).

**Amduat:** title of the most important funerary liturgical work of the New Kingdom, based on the sun's nocturnal journey through the Underworld, divided into twelve sections corresponding to the twelve night hours.

**Amulet:** generally small object intended to protect their owners during their terrestrial lives and in the next world, guaranteeing the conservation of the vital functions and certain qualities (health, wisdom, beauty, etc.).

**Amun:** member of the Theban Triad together with Mut and Khonsu (see). Also known as the "King of the Gods". Depicted in human form, occasionally ithyphallic (see.) or as a ram, with two plumes on his head-dress.

*Ankh:* hieroglyphic symbol of life, a potent amulet.

**Ansate:** referring to vases and receptacles equipped with *ansae*, curved appendixes attached to the sides of vases or amphorae to act as handles or as decoration.

**Anubis:** jackal-headed deity presiding over mummification who escorted the deceased to the next world.

**Apophis:** serpent symbolising the East, vainly attempts to swallow the sun every day at dawn.

**Aten:** the solar disc, depicted with multiple rays ending in hands, imposed by Akhenaten as the sole divinity.

**Atum:** deity representing the sun at dusk, identified as Ra-Atum, demiurge of Heliopolis.

**Bastet:** goddess represented in feline form, with a cat's head or rarely that of a lioness, presides over music and joy.

**Bes:** genius of birth and infants, always depicted from the front and in a threatening pose to defeat evil demons.

*Book of the Dead:* illustrated collection of 190 chapters comprising the formulas that were said to guarantee the survival of the deceased in the underworld.

**Burnisher:** wooden tool, superficially carbonised, used to cover a metal surface with a protective oxide or sulphurous patina, the process being known as burnishing.

**Cachette:** "hiding place", refers in particular to the underground chambers in which royal mummies and parts of the funerary treasures were concealed to protect them from grave robbers.

**Canopic vases:** containers used for the internal organs of the mummified corpse. The funerary furnishings comprised four canopic vases, each of which was placed under the protection of one of the sons of Horus and frequently had a lid representing their features (man, baboon, dog or falcon).

**Cartouche:** oval figure representing a length of cord containing the principal two of the sovereign's five names.

**Criosphinx:** sphinx (see) with a ram's head.

**Crypt:** hypogeum (see) generally dedicated to sacred and funerary functions.

**Demotic:** "relating to the people, popular". Refers to the simplified form of hieroglyphic writing for general use.

**Diorite:** volcanic mineral of a dark colour and exceptional hardness, used in architecture and statuary.

*Dromos:* the avenue giving access to the temples, frequently flanked by sphinxes (see).

**Electrum:** alloy of gold and silver.

**Encaustic:** a painting technique based on the use of pigments dissolved in melted wax and applied hot.

**Faience:** silica paste with a glassy appearance obtained by heating and mixing alkali, copper and sodium; generally takes on a bluish colour.

**Geb:** deity personifying the Earth, husband of Nut (see).

**Gebel:** "mount" in Arabic.

**Ged:** pillar representing the backbone of Osiris and symbolising stability and endurance.

**Harakhty:** see Ra-Harakhty.

**Hathor:** goddess frequently represented with the head of a cow and occasionally with just bovine ears, protected women, music and the deceased.

*Heb-sed:* see Sed.

**Heka-Kasutt:** the "Princes of the Foreign Lands", name given by the Egyptians to the semi-nomadic Semite peoples (or perhaps to their leaders only) who penetrated Egypt in the 17th century BC and were expelled around a century later.

**Hieratic:** "relating to the sacred", within the ambit of ancient Egypt it refers in particular to the simplified transcription of hieroglyphic writing, a kind of cursive script used by priests and functionaries.

**Hieroglyph:** "sacred inscription", each symbol in the ancient Egyptian writing system, originally having an exclusively pictorial and ideographic value, later evolving into a phonetic form.

**Horus:** falcon-headed god, son of Osiris and Isis and nephew of Seth, the principal celestial deity protecting the sovereign and identified with him.

**Horun:** falcon-headed god, locally identified in the sphinx of Giza.

**Hyksos:** Greek transcription of Heka-Kasutt (see).

**Hypogeum:** subterranean.

**Hypostyle:** vast hall with a flat roof supported by rows of columns.

**Iconostasis:** dividing screen typical of Greek Orthodox churches, separates the presbytery from the nave and is lavishly decorated with icons.

**Intercolumniation:** the space between two columns, either empty or occupied by a low wall.

**Ithyphallic:** "of the erect phallus", term relating to the phallic fertility cults.

*Ka:* one of the spirits of man, representing the life force. Created together with the individual, survives the body after death, but depends on the same terrestrial conditions: the offerings of food, real or painted, left in the tombs are destined for the *Ka*, with the individual, survives the body after death, but depends on the same

terrestrial conditions: the offerings of food, real or painted, left in the tombs are destined for the *Ka*.

**Kush:** Egyptian name for Nubia, a territory partly corresponding to resent day northern Sudan.

**Mammisi:** small temples characteristic of the Late Period erected alongside the principal temples and celebrating the birth of a god.

**Mastaba:** the oldest form of Egyptian surface tomb, built in stone or brick. The term means "bench" in Arabic, referring to the parallelepiped form of the building composed of one or more shrines from which the shaft or corridor leading to the underground burial chamber starts.

**Migdol:** fortification of Assyrian origin, the best preserved example of which is found at Western Thebes, in the funerary temple of Rameses III: a fortified gateway of a number of storeys, topped by Assyrian-style stepped battlements.

**Min:** ithyphallic (see) mummiform deity with the right arm raised and gripping a flail; protected the fertility and tracks of the Eastern Desert.

**Montu:** falcon-headed god of war.

**Mut:** bride of Amun, originally a vulture goddess, subsequently took on human form.

*Naos:* the internal part of the temple containing the statue of the divinity.

**Neith:** one of the goddesses of the funerary cult, together with Isis, Nephthys and Selkis. Tutelary divinity, and from the New Kingdom also considered to have given birth to the sun.

*Nemes:* head-dress reserved for the sovereign, consisting of a striped fabric cap with two flaps either side of the face.

**Nephthys:** sister of Isis and consort of Seth, the god who killed Osisris.

**Nilometer:** building containing a graduated pillar destined to measure the level reached by the Nile during the seasonal flood. Its main function was that of calculating in advance the taxable entity of the forthcoming harvest.

**Nomarch:** high ranking functionary governing a nome (see).

**Nome:** administrative area of

ancient Egypt; according to the period, the nomes numbered between 38 and 42.

**Nun**: chaos, the primordial ocean from the waters of which rose the Sky and the Earth.

**Nut**: personification of the celestial vault, bride of Geb (see). Depicted with an arching body and decorated with a cluster of stars.

**Opening of the mouth**: ceremony designed to restore life to the simulacra through the touch of a small instrument representing an axe.

**Opet**: a religious festival held during the third month of the flood: the celebrations focused on the transportation by boat of the statue of Amun from the Temple of Karnak to the Temple of Luxor dedicated to him and known as "Ipet-resit", or Southern Harem (of Amun).

**Osiris**: mummiform god who presided over the Underworld; husband and brother of Isis, killed by his brother Seth and after his death magically generation Horus (see), the falcon-god who avenged him.

*Ostracon*: clay fragment used as a support for brief notes and inscriptions.

*Pronaos*: vestibule of a temple or tomb.

**Ptah**: creator god of Memphis. Depicted as mummiform and bearing a sceptre. Consort of Sekhmet, the lioness goddess, and over the course of time was syncretised with the Memphis funerary deity, Sokaris.

**Punt**: Egyptian name for a territory situated in East Africa (variously identified as Somalia, Eritrea or southern Sudan) towards

which were despatched commercial expeditions from the 5th Dynasty (2465-2323) onwards. The best known expedition was that ordered by Queen Hatshepsut (1479-1458, 18th Dynasty), depicted in a magnificent bas-relief from Deir al-Bahari.

**Pylon**: monumental entrance to the Egyptian temples, composed of two trapezoidal towers either side of a gateway.

*Pyramid texts*: formulas relating to the sovereign's funerary ritual, present in the pyramids from the late 5th Dynasty through to the end of the 6th.

**Pyramidion**: a solar symbol, a miniature pyramid in stone, frequently gilded or covered with electrum (see) and located at the tip of an obelisk or in place of the apex of a pyramid.

**Qasr**: "castle" in Arabic. From the plural noun, *uqsor*, derives the name of Luxor, a corruption of al-Uqsor, "The Castles".

**Ra**: extremely ancient sun deity of Heliopolis. During the day Ra had the head of a falcon overlooked by the solar disc while during his nocturnal journey (see Amduat) he had a ram's head.

**Ra-Horakhty**: syncretic divine figure with the appearance of a falcon and equipped with a solar disc. Unites Ra and Horus in a deity of the two horizons (east and west).

**Rostaw**: indicates in the funerary texts the "paths of the Underworld" followed by the deceased between the fourth and the fifth hours of the night, a sector dominated by Sokar, god of the necropolis of Memphis; in geographical terms, identified the Giza plateau.

*Sacellum*: place of worship in a segregated or hidden room.

**Sanctuary**: the innermost area of the temple, the tabernacle.

*Sarcophagus texts*: collection of formulas intended to guarantee the survival of the deceased in the Underworld, inscribed on the sarcophagi from the First Intermediate Period through to the Middle Kingdom.

**Schist**: metamorphic rock composed of parallel strata.

*Sed*: the jubilee festival celebrated by sovereigns in the thirtieth year of their reign and subsequently at shorter intervals of between five and three years.

**Sekhmet**: lioness goddess, protector of the royal power of the sovereign; occasionally assimilated with Bastet, Hathor and Isis, but possesses a darker connotation than the other goddesses.

**Serapis**: Ptolemaic deity combining the characteristics of Osiris and Olympian attributes, particularly those of the figure of Zeus.

**Seth**: god of chaotic forces, brother and killer of Osiris (see), particularly venerated in the delta. Depicted in human form and with the head of an unrecognisable animal, perhaps an anteater or a greyhound.

*Shawabty*: statuette, frequently made of blue faience (see), destined to replace the owner in the agriculture labours of the Underworld.

**Sistrum**: musical instrument similar to a rattle, sacred to Hathor and Bastet.

**Sobek**: crocodile god, depicted both in human form with the head of the reptile, and in completely animal form.

**Sphinx**: embodiment of royal power with a lion's body and

human male head. Located to guard the doors of temples and along the *dromos* (see).

**Steatite**: compact variety of mineral talcum also known as soapstone. Greenish in colour and easily worked.

**Stela**: stone or wood slab carrying inscriptions and designs linked with the various functions performed: celebratory, funerary, propagandistic and boundary marking.

**Sycamore**: tree sacred to Hathor (see) and Nut (v.); very hard wood used to make furniture, sarcophagi and other funerary accessories.

**Ta-set-Neferu**: ancient Egyptian name for the present day Valley of the Queens variously interpreted as meaning "Place of Beauty", "of Splendours" or "of Lotuses".

*Teken*: Egyptian name for the obelisks.

**Tell**: Arabic term indicating an artificial mound created by the superimposition of the ruins of a settlement.

**Thot**: deity depicted in human form with the head of an ibex or in the form of the bird, or again in the form of a baboon. Protector of scribes and the sciences, considered to be the inventor of writing.

*Udjat*: the eye of Horus, a protective amulet.

**Uraeus**: the cobra, symbol of royalty.

*Wadi*: the dry bed of a stream typical of the desert areas of North Africa and the Near East, flooded only during the seasonal rains. In Arabic, it is close to the term meaning "valley".

**Wadjet**: tutelary goddess of Lower Egypt, takes the form of a *uraeus*.

# Index

# *Illustration credits*

WHITE STAR ARCHIVE: pages 26, 27, 30, 31, 32 bottom, 36 left, 38 bottom right, 38-39, 40, 41 top right, 41 bottom right, 41 bottom left, 42, 43, 47 top, 47 bottom, 56 top, 150, 151, 153 top left, 153.

ANTONIO ATTINI/WHITE STAR ARCHIVE: pages 1, 6 top left, 6 top right, 6 bottom right, 57 top left, 64-65, 68-69, 70 centre, 84 bottom right, 84-85, 85 top, 86 centre, 86 bottom, 87 bottom right, 89 bottom left, 89 bottom right, 104-105, 111 bottom, 114-115, 119 top centre, 120 top, 120 right, 126 bottom, 128-129, 130 top, 130 bottom, 130-131, 131 bottom, 132 bottom, 133 bottom left, 160 top, 162 top, 162 bottom, 164-165, 168, 169, 170 bottom, 171 top, 171 centre, 171 bottom, 172-173, 174 top left, 174 top right, 174 top centre, 174 bottom centre, 174-175, 176 bottom left, 176 bottom right, 176-177, 180 top, 182, 183, 184 bottom right, 184-185, 185 top, 185 bottom left, 185 bottom right, 187 bottom left, 187 bottom right.

MARCELLO BERTINETTI/ WHITE STAR ARCHIVE: pages 6 bottom left, 7, 10-11, 62 centre, 62-63, 66 bottom left, 66-67, 67 top, 68 bottom, 85 bottom, 86 top, 86-87, 90 top, 90 top centre, 90 bottom centre, 90 bottom, 90-91, 108 top, 108 bottom, 108-109, 109 bottom

left, 110 top, 110 centre, 110-111, 112 bottom, 113 top, 113 centre, 113 bottom, 114 top, 114 bottom left, 114 bottom right, 115 top, 115 bottom, 116-117, 122, 123 top, 123 centre, 123 bottom, 123 right, 128 bottom, 130 centre, 131 centre, 132-133, 133 bottom right, 135 top left, 135 top right, 135 centre, 135 bottom, 136 bottom left, 136-137, 137 top, 137 centre, 137 bottom, 138 bottom, 139 top, 140 centre, 146 bottom left, 146 bottom right, 184 bottom left.

ARALDO DE LUCA/WHITE STAR ARCHIVE: pages 5, 12, 13, 14, 15, 16, 17, 18, 19, 20, 21, 22, 23, 25, 28, 29, 32 top, 32 centre left, 32 centre right, 33, 36 bottom, 36 right, 37, 60, 61, 70 top, 70 bottom, 70-71, 71 bottom left, 72, 73, 74, 75, 76, 77, 78, 79, 80, 81, 82, 83, 123 bottom left, 124, 125, 136 bottom right, 139 bottom right, 139 bottom, 140 top left, 140 bottom, 141, 142 bottom left, 142-143, 143 top, 143 bottom, 144 top, 144 centre, 144 bottom, 144-145, 147 top, 147 bottom, 149 top, 149 bottom, 152, 156 top, 156 centre, 156 bottom, 156-157.

ALFIO GAROZZO/WHITE STAR ARCHIVE: pages 56 bottom left, 56 bottom right, 57 top right, 57 bottom right, 58, 59, 70 top centre, 84 bottom left, 92, 93, 94, 95, 96 top, 96 bottom, 97 bottom,

98, 99, 104 top, 128 top, 138 centre, 138-139, 148 bottom left, 148 bottom right, 48-149, 154-155, 158, 159, 161 bottom, 166, 167, 172 top, 172 centre, 172 bottom, 174 bottom, 175 centre, 175 bottom.

GIULIO VEGGI/WHITE STAR ARCHIVE: pages 2-3, 4, 54, 55, 62 top, 62 bottom, 64 bottom left, 64 bottom right, 65, 66 bottom centre, 67 top, 67 bottom, 68 top, 86 bottom left, 87 bottom left, 88 top, 88 bottom, 88-89, 100, 101, 102 bottom left, 102 bottom right, 102-103, 103 right, 104 centre, 104 bottom, 105 bottom left, 105 bottom right, 106 and 107, 109 bottom right, 112-113, 116, 117 top, 118-119, 119 top, 119 bottom centre, 119 bottom, 120 centre, 120 bottom, 121, 126 top, 132 top, 134, 138 top, 140 top right, 145 bottom, 146-147, 160 bottom, 160-161, 161 top, 162-163, 163 bottom left, 163 bottom right, 164 top, 164 centre, 164 bottom, 165 bottom, 170-171, 177 top, 177 bottom, 178 bottom left, 178 bottom right, 178-179, 179 top, 179 bottom, 180 left centre, 180 bottom, 180 right, 181.

FELIPE ALCOCEBA: page 71 bottom right.

BIBLIOTECA NAZIONALE, FIRENZE: page 38 bottom left.

BRITISH MUSEUM: page 35.

PRIVATE COLLECTION: pages 39 bottom, 44, 45 top left, 45 bottom left, 45 bottom right.

MARC DEVILLE: pages 96-97.

GRIFFITH INSTITUTE ASHMOLEAN MUSUM, OXFORD: pages 49, 50, 51.

ARCHIVE PAUL LACAU: page 48 bottom.

LIBRARY OF CONGRESS, WASHINGTON: pages 46 bottom left, 46 bottom right, 46-47.

MARY EVANS PICTURE LIBRARY: page 48 top left.

MUSÉE D'ANNECY: page 45 top right.

MUSÉE DENON, CHALON SUR SAÔNE: page 38 top.

GARO NALBANDIAN: page 187 centre.

NASA: pages 8 and 9.

PLAILLY/EURELIOS: pages 96 left top, 96 left centre.

ALBERTO SILIOTTI: pages 34, 41 top left, 41 centre, 48 centre, 48 right, 142 bottom right.

**Cover**
*One of the two colossus statues of Ramses II that stand either side of the entrance to the Temple of Luxor can be seen behind the only surviving obelisk.*
*Photograph by Marcello Bertinetti/White Star Archive*

**Back cover, top left**
*St. Catherine's Monastery stands at the foot of Gebel Musa, the biblical Mount Sinai.*
*Photograph by Antonio Attini/White Star Archive*

**Back cover, top right**
*Queen Nefertari reciting a verse from the Book of the Dead before the ibis-headed god Thoth.*

*Decoration from the queen's tomb in the Valley of the Queens.*
*Photograph by White Star Archive*

**Back cover, bottom left**
*Tutankhamen, the young "golden pharaoh", appears to relive in the opulence of his funerary mask.*
*Egyptian Museum of Cairo.*
*Photograph by Araldo De Luca/White Star Archive*

**Back cover, bottom right**
*The enigmatic face of the Great Sphinx at Giza portrays the pharaoh Khafre, son of Khufu and occupant of the necropolis' second pyramid.*
*Photograph by Giulio Veggi/White Star Archive*